The Social Market Foundatio
The Foundation's main activi
publish original papers by inc
experts on key topics in the ec
a view to stimulating public discussion on the performance of
markets and the social framework within which they operate.
The Foundation is a registered charity and a company limited
by guarantee. It is independent of any political party or group
and is financed by the sale of publications and by voluntary
donations from individuals, organisations and companies.
The views expressed in publications are those of the authors
and do not represent a corporate opinion of the Foundation.

Chairman
David Lipsey (Lord Lipsey of Tooting Bec)

Members of the Board
Viscount Chandos
Gavyn Davies
David Edmonds
Daniel Finkelstein
John McFadden
Brian Pomeroy

Director
Ann Rossiter

First published by
The Social Market Foundation,
February 2006

The Social Market Foundation
11 Tufton Street
London SW1P 3QB

Designed by Paula Snell Design

Contents

Acknowledgements

Many people have been instrumental in providing valuable feedback on this project. We would like to thank the main authors – Sarah Smith, Alissa Goodman, Peter Smith, and Stephen Bailey for contributing chapters and for their presentations at the two seminars held during the course of 2005. The SMF would also like to thank the following external reviewers for their help in developing the critique in this collection: Deborah Rozansky, Health Foundation; Professor Nick Barr, LSE; Tom Startup, Deloitte; Niall Maclean, SMF; Saranjit Sihota, Office for Public Services Reform; Sara Apps, Which?; and Theo Blackwell, Camden Council. Thank you also to Ben Page, Director of the Social Research Institute at MORI, whose presentation at the first co-payments seminar helped to set our work firmly in the context of public acceptance of charges. Lastly, thanks to Sanofi Pasteur MSD for supporting the seminars and a stimulating dinner at the Labour Party Conference 2005, and Dave Roberts at Munro & Forster for his assistance throughout the whole project.

Introduction

Jessica Asato, Researcher, Social Market Foundation

This collection of essays and case studies seeks to inform debate on the use of co-payments and user charges in UK public services. The SMF organised two seminars in 2005, the first investigated the rationale for public service co-payments, and the second looked at situations in which we might contemplate the introduction or extension of co-payments. We invited four of our speakers to prepare chapters based on their presentations which we include in this publication covering the economics of co-payment, user charges in health care, fees in higher education and charges in local government. The following introduction sets out the main arguments raised in the subsequent chapters, looks at the rationale for co-payments and reflects upon some of the issues raised in the seminars. The three case studies included at the end of this collection provide practical examples of new areas for the possible extension of co-payments.

What are co-payments?
The terms co-payment, co-financing, cost sharing, user charge, and user fee tend to be used interchangeably in political debate which can cause confusion. The main difference between co-payment and a user charge or fee is that co-payment refers to the model of public service funding (from both state and individual contributions simultaneously), whereas user charges or fees can apply where there is no corresponding state contribution (some waste collection services for example). A distinction could also be drawn between co-payments which are shared with the state for a general service (such as prescriptions), and co-payments which enable service users to access top-up services (such as private hospital rooms in the NHS).

This publication refers both to co-payments and user charges, though in the future, we consider that the term 'shared contributions' may be a clearer way of explaining the principle to the public.[1]

The political context

Public services may be funded either through taxes (or social insurance in many countries) or through charges levied on individuals and employers. All countries use some form of co-payment in the delivery of public services. The extent of co-payment, however, very much depends on the historical political settlement and the culture of the country in question. It is likely that the wide public acceptance of co-payment in the Swedish healthcare system, for example, is in part due to the fact that before the introduction of co-payments in 1970, the public already had to meet high out-of-pocket expenses. In the UK, the development of the welfare state through Beveridge and the 1945 Labour Government has meant there has been less of a central role for co-payment, though there are notable exceptions.[2] The introduction of charges has tended to be a result of political expediency, rather than to have been introduced on a principled, well thought out basis. Prescription charges, for example, were introduced by Hugh Gaitskell ostensibly to fund increased arms expenditure. It is telling that debate about the use of charges for public services has tended to surface at times of constraints on public spending, notably in the early 1980s and 1990s. As a result, the use of co-payment in the UK follows no logical pattern.

In the foreseeable future, an uncertain economic climate and budget deficits may force policy makers to once again consider the introduction of new, or the extension of existing, user charges. For example, Stephen Byers suggested that co-payments could be introduced into less essential services such as support of the elderly, meals-on-wheels, and missed GP appointments, in a speech he made to the SMF[3]. He did, however, stress that no charges or co-payments should be introduced into essential services such as the NHS and schools – an approach which has been backed up by John Reid who, as Secretary of State for Health, ruled out any new charges in the NHS.[4] Tony Blair has also suggested that co-payment in areas

1 As suggested by Ben Page from MORI at the Social Market Foundation seminar on 4th March 2005 *Filling the black hole? The use of co-payment in UK public services.*

2 Prescription charges, for example, were introduced very early on, in 1948, and other charges exist in many, usually local government, services (see Stephen Bailey's chapter for more examples of local government charges).

3 Speech on Public Service Reform, 28th May 2003.

4 http: //www.guardian.co.uk/ guardianpolitics/story/0,,114 8878,00.html

5 Question to Tony Blair in the House of Commons Liaison Committee: Tuesday 3 February 2004.

6 *User Charging in the Federal Government – A Background Document*, (1997) Treasury Board of Canada, Secretariat

which are not 'core' public services should be looked at in the long-term.[5] However, there is little political analysis to inform policy development on co-payment, and a lack of understanding of the rationale for, and effects of, co-payments on service delivery. Consequently there has been little investigation of how a system of co-payment might work in areas of UK public services today, or whether co-payments could be used to fund the introduction of new services.[6]

When might it be suitable to introduce user charges?

In the case of certain public sector activities, it is clear that they cannot and should not be financed by user charges (the armed forces, for example). In many other instances though, whether co-payment should be introduced is subject to ideological debate. Other governments have sought to ground decisions in a transparent framework. A report for the Canadian Government, for example, sought to establish whether or not a service should be subject to charges based on the characteristics of the activities in question and the nature of the market for the service.

That report identified six characteristics that indicate whether user charges may be appropriate or not:

1. "Rivalness" – the more one person's consumption of a service affects another's level of consumption, the more desirable in efficiency terms it is to charge for it.
2. Excludability – purely public goods and services should not prevent a person from using the good/service if they can't pay for it.
3. Economies of scale.
4. Sunkenness of costs – given the sheer scale of some infrastructure projects, certain public sector activities should be provided by the state because it may be difficult for the private sector if it is unlikely to recover full costs.
5. Externalities – Some services give rise to important public benefits that are hard to price and make it difficult to charge for (e.g. education). Others (such as transport) may generate benefits that can be priced, which could be charged for. Negative externalities (such as pollution) can also be charged for.
6. Social/political objectives – it seems obvious, but a system

of charging must fit with political objectives. If the sole objective of a particular policy is redistribution, it would not make sense to charge beneficiaries according to the benefits they receive, but it may do if they were charged according to income.

What is the rationale for co-payment?
There are a number of reasons why co-payments may be used in public services: to restrict demand; to increase revenue; as an alternative to raising general taxation; to create greater equity; and to bolster support for core public services. Some of these stand up to scrutiny better than others. Taking each of these in turn:

a) To restrict demand
The most frequently used rationale for the introduction of user fees is to prevent over-consumption and to make the public's use of services more responsible.[7] Economic theory suggests that free public services lead people to over-consume.[8] This was backed up by a major study by the RAND think tank in the US (discussed in Peter Smith's essay) which compared healthcare demand under a free-care plan and a user-fee plan.[9] The study found that *"use of medical services responds unequivocally to changes in the amount paid out of pocket"*- expenses were up to 45% higher for the free-care individuals compared to those who had user fees.

User fees reduce excess demand by putting the service user in the driving seat, giving them a clearer idea of the cost of a particular service and how their money pays for it. A service user is more likely to be price-conscious if they are directly paying for a service rather than receiving a universally tax-funded service. Co-payment can therefore help to prevent waste and encourage service users to better engage with the service they are paying for.

b) To increase revenue
A closely associated issue is the need government may have to increase revenue for public services. This may be caused by a number of factors: the ageing population, technological advances, increasing staff costs, etc. Financing public services through general taxation is likely to become more difficult as

7 See for example the reason given by Socialstyrelsen (The National Board of Health & Welfare) in Sweden for their use of user charges: http://www.sos.se/full-text/111/2002-111-1/summary.htm

8 See Feldstein, M. S. (1973). *The welfare loss of excess health insurance.* The Journal of Political Economy 81(2): 251-80.

9 The RAND Health Insurance Experiment (HIE) involved approx. 2000 non-elderly families and ran from 1974 to 1982.

10 Appelby & Boyle (2000)
*Blair's billions: where will he
find the money for the NHS?*
BMJ, 2000, 320, pp. 865-7

11 Derek Wanless (April 2002)
*Securing Our Future Health:
Taking A Long-Term View*, HM
Treasury

12 Derek Wanless (February
2004) *Securing Good Health
for the Whole Population*, HM
Treasury

13 *Future demand for long-
term care in the UK: A summary
of projections of long-term care
finance for older people to
2051* Raphael Wittenberg,
Adelina Comas-Herrera, Linda
Pickard and Ruth Hancock,
published by the Joseph
Rowntree Foundation
September 2004

14 Vidhya Alakeson (October
2004) *A 2020 vision for early
years: extending choice;
improving life chances*, SMF

15 Health policy & economic
research unit, BMA; (1997)
Options for funding health care.

people's demands on public services increase. For example, it has been argued that to maintain spending on healthcare at EU levels we would have to increase the basic rate of income tax by 2p per year, or carry out an immediate increase in VAT from 17.5% to 27%.[10] Derek Wanless in his report on health spending for the Treasury argued that a tax funded NHS would only be feasible under a 'fully-engaged' scenario where people take an active role in getting healthier and more money is diverted into prevention.[11] More recently, in his report on achieving this scenario, Wanless has admitted that this is going to be a difficult and potentially impossible task.[12]

The same pressures exist in social care. It has been estimated that long-term care spending in the UK would need to rise by around 315% in real terms between 2000 and 2051 to meet demographic pressures and allow for real rises in care costs if dependency rates, patterns of care and funding arrangements remain unchanged.[13] Similarly, spending on childcare will need to rise in order to cope with increased parental participation in the workforce and demands for better quality childcare. To meet the SMF's vision for early years in 2020, for example, PricewaterhouseCoopers estimated that spending would have to increase by around 1.8% of GDP (c.£21 billion at 2004/5 values) on current spending levels.[14]

Co-payment is attractive because it has the potential to raise some of the additional revenue needed to maintain high quality public services without raising general taxation. In healthcare, for example, it has been estimated that 'hotel charges' of £40 per day in hospital would raise £1.25bn (if there were no exemptions) and a £10 GP consultation could raise £3.3bn.[15] Advocates of co-payment in healthcare point to low waiting lists and a lack of shortage of healthcare professionals in some systems of co-payment (such as the social insurance systems used in France and the Netherlands).

We have to be careful, however, about expecting co-payment to always substantially increase the funding available for public services, particularly given the need to consider equity issues. While user fees may deter people from using public services unnecessarily, they may at the same time discourage necessary use. This has led to many systems of co-payment developing quite wide or complex exemptions which can reduce the sums generated considerably.[16] Exemptions on equity grounds (for example giving prescriptions free to those on lower incomes) may result in low overall returns from the charge.

In addition, if co-payments dissuade people from using a service, there may be costs to public services further down the line. For example, a low-uptake of prescriptions may result in conditions worsening, which may then require even more expensive treatment. Even though the use of co-payment in Swedish healthcare has been publicly accepted since the 1970s, it still only generates about 2% of healthcare funding. The amount of revenue raised by a particular user charge, therefore, will depend on the design of the co-payment system and it is important to model the secondary effects of co-payment.

c) As an alternative to general taxation
Advocates of user charges might see their role as going beyond raising additional funding for public services and instead argue for charges as a substitute for general taxation. This might be the case in those instances where user charges may bring additional social or environmental benefits when compared with general taxation – for example, road user charging. It can also be argued that the British public are unlikely to accept further tax increases in the near future (though this may be exaggerated, see the discussion below). If people are expected to pay more for services they will want to see a more direct relationship between the money they pay and the outcome for themselves.[17] It has been argued that it was for this reason that the Labour Government's increase in National Insurance was acceptable: it was semi-hypothecated for the NHS. What is gained in public acceptance through using hypothecation, however, may be lost in flexibility over future budgets. Moreover, this poses a challenge to the consensus on collectively funded public services, leading to a potentially difficult situation if the public start to demand that they should only pay for that which they directly benefit from.

d) To create greater equity
Once again, depending on the design, co-payment can be redistributive, thereby creating a more equitable system. For example, modelling by the Institute for Fiscal Studies showed

16 Emmerson and Reed (2003) *Use of fees in the provision of public services in OECD countries*

17 This was the conclusion of the Fabian Society Commission on Taxation and Citizenship 2000. In opinion polling carried out for the project they found that around 40% of people supported an increase of 1p on the basic rate of income tax for unspecified public spending. This rose when the spending area was specified (68% for education, and 80% for health).

18 Emmerson and Reed chapter 6 *Alternatives for Welfare Policy: Coping with Internationalisation and Demographic Change* Torben M. Andersen (Editor), Per Molander (Editor) 2003

that higher education fees were generally redistributive because graduates tended to earn higher salaries.[18] Alongside proposed higher education (HE) payments in the UK is a system of maintenance loans and subsidy for the poorest students so that the effect of user charges is partially mitigated. This further enables the system to be redistributive by not penalising poorer students with higher loan repayments once they have graduated. For further discussion of this, see Alissa Goodman's chapter on HE funding.

Co-payment for childcare can also be more redistributive if wealthier parents pay a higher share of childcare costs, enabling the state to pay for poorer children. If the objective of increasing childcare provision is for reasons of child development, however, it may be that the co-payment system needs to combine elements of redistribution with universal provision for some elements.

User charges for transport can be quite punitive for lower income groups, if the objective of user charging is to reduce car use rather than primarily to raise revenue. This is because in order to dampen demand for car use, the charge has to be reasonably high – which has a disproportionate effect on those on lower incomes. Schemes that are designed to raise revenue, however, tend to be characterised by relatively low charges. With flat rate charges, the negative effect on those from lower income backgrounds can be overcome by introducing exemptions. For example, the congestion charge in London is not payable by key workers and disabled badge holders. Tailoring the exemptions more accurately to lower income groups, however, can be administratively expensive. In the long-term, the aim should be to overcome equity considerations by improving public transport to the level where it becomes an attractive alternative to the car.

e) To bolster public support for core public services
People's expectations of public services means that the public sector will have to continue to look at increasing user choice and introducing more flexibility and personalisation into the services it delivers. Co-payments may, in some cases, help this process by giving users increased options over the services they receive. Peter Smith suggests in his essay, for example, that by

enabling people to pay for health interventions on the periphery, support for a tax-funded 'statutory core package' may increase. Case Study One also puts forward an interesting proposal which would enable older women to co-pay for a new cervical cancer vaccine, while those girls between 12 and 16, who would benefit it most, would be given the vaccine free on the NHS. If people can 'top-up' the tax-funded services they currently receive, it is argued that they are less likely to turn to the private sector. As Sarah Smith points out, however, the opposite may result if the public is increasingly expected to pay for things in the public sector that they could equally receive in the private. Much of this depends on the extent to which the public will accept the need to pay twice for services.

19 2004 Commonwealth Fund International Health Policy Survey of Adults' Experiences with Primary Care

A general rationale?

As we have seen, there can be a number of reasons why policy makers may favour co-payments in a particular service. A general rationale may run as follows:

'Co-payments in public services can in some circumstances help to reduce demand, generate additional revenue, increase efficiency, and can be redistributive. Co-payments must, however, take into consideration the principles of equity and public acceptability if they are to be viable in the UK system of public services.'

The main arguments against increased co-payment

The strongest argument against the use of co-payment in public services is that it penalises lower income groups and prevents take-up of vital services. Most of the evidence comes from the use of co-payments in healthcare. In France the *Couverture Maladie Universelle* was introduced because there was evidence that relatively high co-payments for many outpatient services tended to discourage the poor from seeking care. A major study undertaken by the Commonwealth Fund compared people's lack of access to primary health services due to cost.[19] They found that 4% of respondents in the UK said they did not fill prescriptions or skipped doses compared to 22% in the US, and 4% had a medical problem but did not visit their doctor in the UK, compared to 29% in the US. Moreover, there was a much stronger effect on adults with below average incomes – in the UK 12% of poorer people went without needed care due

20 National Association of
Citizens Advice Bureaux (2001)
Unhealthy charges: CAB evidence of the impact of health charges

21 See: http://www.sos.se/fulltext/111/2002-111-1/summary.htm

22 See Jones, P. (2001)
Addressing Equity Concerns in Relation to Road User Charging
Transport Studies Group,
University of Westminster

to the costs, compared to 9% of all adults, and in the US it was much higher – 57% of poorer adults, compared to 40% of adults as a whole. The negative effect on access in the US was mainly put down to high uninsured rates and cost-sharing, while the UK showed "negligible cost-related access problems" because of the historically low rates of co-payment.

In the UK the Citizens Advice Bureau has provided evidence showing that prescription, dental and optical charges put off people on low incomes from seeking treatment, particularly those with long-term health problems.[20] According to the Swedish National Board of Health & Welfare, in 1999 just over 3% of the population abstained from healthcare because of the size of user charges, around 4% from purchasing pharmaceuticals, and 15% from dental care. Younger people tended to be deterred to a greater extent than older people. One in six older people in need of assistance abstained from home help, for which there is a substantial user charge that varies widely among municipalities. Individuals with low incomes were more likely to do without services in general.[21] Similar arguments have been made to oppose the introduction of road user charging[22], and continued charges for social care.

It should be noted that user charges may have other knock on effects that do not directly affect the user or potential user. Congestion charges, for example, can affect businesses within the charging zone. Compensatory schemes, however, can be designed alongside user charges to offset losses in some instances. Businesses may receive increased investment in their

In the UK the Citizens Advice Bureau has provided evidence showing that prescription, dental and optical charges put off people on low incomes from seeking treatment, particularly those with long-term health problems.

area to increase its attractiveness to potential shoppers and offset the potential loss in custom through a congestion charge. Tyne and Wear Council has announced that it will use part of its revenues raised through the recently announced road pricing pilot to compensate local businesses which lose out because of the charge.

As has already been pointed out in relation to general taxation in higher education, there are some instances in which a co-payment may be *more* equitable than general taxation – it depends on the user charge in question. Studies such as the RAND Health Insurance Experiment (see Peter Smith's chapter for further discussion on this) concluded that while there was some evidence that the user fees impacted negatively on the health of some groups (mainly poor people with blood pressure, and those who were poor and already in bad health), this could be rectified by exempting these users from fees. Once again this shows that while there are obvious impacts on equity, this need not necessarily be the case once equity is taken into consideration in the design of the co-payment system.

Other opposition to co-payments tends to relate to the impact they may have on the nature of the UK welfare system. For example, some commentators see the increase of co-payment as the precursor of privatisation.[23] While it is true that countries which rely more heavily on private finance tend to be less progressive,[24] co-payments need not necessarily detract from the overall proportion of public services financed through taxation. Moreover, since one of the arguments for co-payment is to attract middle class support for public services by offering enhanced or better quality services, it is not the case that greater use of co-payments necessarily paves the way for a reduced role for public services.

A practical argument against co-payment is that the administration costs, particularly with wide exemption schemes, reduce the impact of the charge both in regards to its revenue raising ability and also its potential for reducing demand. While it is indeed true that co-payment systems are often administratively complex, this can be outweighed by the amount raised by the charge. For example, the Social Market Foundation Health Commission ruled out abolishing prescription charges altogether because the £400 million that would be lost

23 See Pollock, A. (October 2004) NHS Plc: *The Privatisation of Our Health Care*

24 See Propper, C. Green, C. (April 1999) *A Larger Role For The Private Sector In Health Care? A Review Of The Arguments* CMPO, University of Bristol http://www.bris.ac.uk/Depts/CMPO/workingpapers/wp9.pdf

25 For further discussion see also: The Sutton Trust, (June 2005) *No More School Run: Proposal for a national yellow bus scheme in the UK*

from the NHS as a result is a significant sum of money. There may also be additional savings generated from co-payment schemes that are less easy to quantify. For example, were there to be an expansion of home-to-school transport, as is proposed in Case Study Two co-payments would not only raise money to cover the costs of the transport, the system would also help to facilitate a move from cars on the school run to buses. This would give rise to potential savings through parents being able to spend extra time at work and savings to other road users from having less congested roads.[25]

Where next for co-payments in the UK?

The essays included in this collection have been commissioned in order to contribute to our knowledge of the effects of co-payments in the UK and to investigate whether there is scope for increasing their use in public services.

The first essay by Sarah Smith concentrates on the effects of co-payments on efficiency and equity in public services. She argues that the primary effect of introducing a charge on services which have previously been free and un-rationed is likely to be to reduce demand for that service. In some cases, this is exactly what is desired. Smith uses the congestion charge as an example of using a charge to reflect negative social costs; in this case, those associated with congestion. This should result in drivers switching to public transport, or choosing to drive at non-peak times, as the charge is added to the private costs they bear. If charges are adopted for public services such as health and education, however, which typically have positive social benefits, then setting the level of charge too high will result in the service being under-consumed. This analysis leads to the conclusion that charges are useful for purposes of efficiency where there is clear "excess demand", but that charges can be less efficient in situations where an increase in uptake of services is desirable.

Sarah Smith outlines the distributional consequences of charges. She argues these are straightforward: charging for a service which is used more by lower income groups (e.g. healthcare) is more regressive than charging for services used more by higher income groups (e.g. higher education). Though she points out that even though a charge may be designed to attach to the middle-class user, it may still restrict access for those on lower incomes. Smith next considers the impact of charging on the supply of public services. She argues that as long as revenue from charges, supplements rather than replaces tax revenue, they should allow an increase in the supply of services that are currently rationed. Charges can work like hypothecated taxes – reassuring the citizen that their money is being spent on the services they want and making the use of funding more transparent compared to the current system of taxation. However, additional revenue from charges is only likely to be generated in public services which do not have high levels of low income users. This leads her to consider the possibility of differentiating between core and periphery levels of service provision – a theme which is developed further in chapter three by Peter Smith. In this case, the core service would be provided free to all, while the periphery service could only be accessed by paying a charge.

This raises a number of issues, including whether creating such a system would be likely to increase middle-class demand for public services and therefore reduce the availability of resources overall for less well-off groups. There is also a possibility that support for the welfare state will wane if the better-off are increasingly expected to pay for services twice, and particularly if those same services are available at a similar cost and quality in the private sector. Smith concludes that greater understanding of the links between public support for publicly-funded services and their willingness to pay extra will be crucial when considering the extension of user charges.

The next three essays look more specifically at the use of co-payment in higher education, healthcare and local government. Alissa Goodman argues that the original rationale for introducing top-up fees in higher education (HE) – which was to raise extra revenue – was inadequate, and that the argument should have instead been made on the grounds of equity or efficiency. She then proceeds to assess whether charges for HE could indeed be successful in creating more efficiency and equity. Goodman argues that government intervention in the HE sector on efficiency grounds is necessary because individuals in a private market would fail to take account of the social returns to investment in HE. This does not justify a 100% taxpayer subsidy in her view, however, because of the large private returns to participation in HE. Quoting research by the Institute for Fiscal Studies, she suggests women receive between 25% to 27% higher earnings as a result of going into HE. This could amount to an average of £200,000 more than someone who did not go into HE, which is a substantial amount compared to the average cost of a three year degree – £9,000. This makes a reasonable case, therefore, for the introduction of some level of charge to better reflect the private gains from HE.

Efficiency gains could be made because of the potential for price competition within the sector. Goodman argues that the efficiency gains from the differential fee, however, are unlikely to be gained in practice because most universities have stated they will charge the full fee. She suggests that this fact, alongside the substantial personal benefit of a university degree, provides the rationale for the lifting of the cap on top-up fees when it comes up for review in 2010. Goodman looks next at the impact of top-up fees on low income students, and its possible effects on equity. She argues that concerns about equity in relation to the poorest students are misplaced because of the substantial package of compensation through grants and bursaries. However, students from the lower to middle end of the income distribution scale may be put off attending HE, and this is something that the Government should be concerned about because they represent part of the group of students being targeted for increased attendance at university. Despite these concerns, however, Goodman concludes that raising revenue through the current system of top-up fees is more progressive than if the same amount had been taken from general taxation.

In his essay Peter Smith considers user charges in healthcare and suggests there are two uses of charges: the first is to raise finance, and the second is to dissuade patients from unnecessarily utilising healthcare. In reference to the latter, Smith looks at a RAND experiment which showed consistent reductions in the utilisation of healthcare amongst all groups tested as the cost of charges increased. For most of the population the experiment succeeded in encouraging less profligate use of healthcare without any subsequent serious health consequences. A major exception to this, however, was the seriously adverse effect of charges on those who were poor and suffering from poor health. Peter Smith suggests this raises tensions between the equity goal of universal access and the efficiency goal of ensuring the necessary use of health services. Despite this, he argues that looking at the increased use of charges is imperative in the face of the increasing pace of technological innovation and the rise in patient demands. He concludes that a major rethink of the use of charges in healthcare is required because future healthcare systems will become increasingly financially unsustainable.

This reasoning leads Smith to propose a system of health-care which has a core of health interventions and technologies paid by the taxpayer – "the statutory package". NICE (the National Institute for Health & Clinical Excellence) would be given an expanded remit to decide the scope of the package. Charges could then be levied on interventions which fell outside this package. Moreover, technologies which fail on the grounds of cost-effectiveness could still be included in the core package by NICE but at a subsidised price, giving patients more choice over the treatments they can receive. Smith agrees that this system would have to be accompanied by a comprehensive system of exemptions for poorer groups and certain categories of patients to ensure equity of access. He concludes that the alternative – persisting with the status quo – would lead governments to reduce the NHS in scope and quality because of financial necessity, which would eventually result in the loss of widespread support for a tax-funded NHS.

The final chapter, by Stephen Bailey, looks at the current use of charges in local government and proposes some areas in which they could be extended. Bailey argues that charges are

---

charging has a key role to play in helping to deliver Best Value in councils and in encouraging citizens to use local services more responsibly.

---

26 Robinson, P. (2004) *How do we pay? Funding public services in Europe*, IPPR

more than just a mechanism for revenue generation or for curbing demand – a common theme throughout the essays. He suggests that charges in local government can also serve as a signal of demand, and that they can inform members of the public about the true cost of public service provision. Despite the benefits of user charges at a local level, however, Bailey shows that local government charges have historically been developed on an ad hoc basis and that there is no uniform national policy for such charges. He argues that a new focus on local charges could play a role in the 'recasting' of the welfare state so that the relationship between citizen and state is one of mutual responsibility, not paternalism.

Bailey suggests a number of areas within local government where the use of charges could be expanded to improve service quality and efficiency. For example, housing authorities could levy increased charges for concierge services and extra cleaning; locally determined planning charges could help councils to recover infrastructure costs relating to physical development; road-user charges could help cut congestion and pay for roads; charges for collection of household waste based on volume could encourage citizens to recycle more; charges for personal training coaches in council leisure facilities could contribute to local health targets; charges for policing in city centres at night could combat anti-social behaviour; and an increase in school meal charges could help councils achieve the new *Healthy Eating Blueprint*. In conclusion, Bailey argues that charging has a key role to play in helping to deliver Best Value in councils and in encouraging citizens to use local services more responsibly.

Conclusions

Peter Robinson has argued that the key principle for deciding whether, and in what ways, user charges should be used, is if they help to advance key public policy outcomes.[26] He suggests that revenue raising should *not* be the primary justification for a greater use of user charging, although it is unlikely that revenue raising (certainly as a political justification) can be avoided in a political discussion about co-payment. Robinson also concludes that the lack of clear ideological patterns in the incidence of user charging in Europe means that any further moves to

introduce or extend user charging should be firmly based on
evidence and have a clear rationale.

Public acceptability will also play a large part in considering whether to increase charges or introduce new ones. There is
some discrepancy between recorded public attitudes towards
raising taxation, and political perceptions of whether this is
reflected in reality. When it comes to financing the welfare state
through taxation, *British Social Attitudes* surveys have shown
that large proportions of the public – between 80% and 88% –
felt it was mainly the government's responsibility to pay for
healthcare for the sick.[27] Similarly, a survey by MORI in 2004
found that 61% of the public supported the comment "Public
services such as health and education should be funded by the
taxpayer and be available free at the point of use to all
citizens".[28] Moreover, when asked whether they would be willing to pay higher taxes for public services, a majority of people
have agreed that there should be an increase in taxes every year
since 1987. In 2003 51% of people agreed that 'if the
Government had to choose, it should increase taxes and spend
more'.[29] Politicians are quite sceptical, however, about whether
the public are willing to translate this apparent enthusiasm for
taxation into votes at the ballot box. As David Lipsey has
pointed out, "it is *other* people's taxes, not their own, that they
have in mind – say 'the rich' or tax dodgers or large companies."[30]
If it can be demonstrated that the public are not in favour of
increasing general taxation for a particular service, user charges
may be a more acceptable form of payment.

There is also evidence that the public must believe that the
Government *needs* the money in order to support rises in taxation,
and presumably one would assume charges too. A MORI
survey carried out just after the fuel tax crisis in 2000 found
that 73% supported the statement "Government can afford to
cut petrol taxes as it has enough money in reserve to maintain
spending on public services, such as schools and hospitals".[31] It
is also important that any revenue from tax rises, or additional
charges, are seen to go directly into the particular service in
question. Ben Page from MORI pointed out in an SMF seminar
on co-payment in March 2005 that the public are more willing
to accept an extension of existing charging schemes, but are
wary of the introduction of new schemes. For example, the

27 As quoted in Bochel, H. & Defty, A. (2005) *Public & Parliamentary Attitudes to Welfare.* http://www.psa.ac.uk/2005/ps/Bochel.pdf

28 As cited in presentation by Ben Page to the Social Market Foundation seminar on 4th March 2005 *Filling the black hole? The use of co-payment in UK public services*

29 As quoted in Bochel, H. and Defty, A. (2005) *Public & Parliamentary Attitudes to Welfare.* http://www.psa.ac.uk/2005/ps/Bochel.pdf

30 ibid.

31 See the article by Ben Page, (5th July 2002) *Better Services = More Tax?* http://www.mori.com/mrr/2002/c020705.shtml

32 ibid.

33 See discussion of this in Cowley, P. (2005) *The Rebels: How Blair Mislaid His Majority*

34 See: *Make the Sick Pay,* The Telegraph, 1st December 2005 http://www.telegraph.co.uk/money/main.jhtml?xml=/money/2005/12/01/cngsk01.xml&menuld=242&sSheet=/money/2005/12/01/ixcitytop.html

35 See http://education.guardian.co.uk/policy/story/0,15572,1505457,00.html

public feel generally quite negative about NHS parking charges, but put up with them because parking is charged for in other spheres. People are also more likely to support charges or increased taxes if they think that they will be spent efficiently and competently.[32] As Ben Page argues, this is the reason why Labour won in 1997, rather than their general commitment not to raise income tax; the opposite of which has been widely seen as the reason why Neil Kinnock lost in 1992.

Last of all, if politicians are going to be successful in winning public support for increased or new charges, they will have to show bold leadership and some demonstrable early wins. Ken Livingstone's congestion charge is a case in which communication of the reasons for the charge was key to its eventual acceptance. The case for top-up fees provides the opposite example, where the debate lacked a convincing public service rationale. If Labour politicians had articulated the case for top-up fees on the basis of equity, rather than finance, they may have had more success convincing the Parliamentary Labour Party and the public at large.[33]

Recent calls to introduce charging have ranged from the Chief Executive of GlaxoSmithKline arguing that extra charges are necessary to fund future drugs[34] to the consideration of charges to fund extended schools.[35] The following set of essays conclude that there may be further room for the use of co-payments in the UK, but that the question of equity must be at the forefront of public policy makers' minds when considering extending current charges or introducing new ones.

User charging: some efficiency and equity implications

Sarah Smith,[36] **Centre for Market & Public Organisation and Department of Economics, University of Bristol**

In the real world, public opinion and historical context are crucial in determining which public services people are charged for and which they get for free. It would be a brave – and likely short-lived – politician who proposed charging for a popular service that people currently enjoy free at the point of use, simply because it is economically efficient. But the economics of user charging cannot be ignored. Whether a public service is paid for out of general taxation or by the end-user inevitably affects demand and supply, as well as how the burden of the cost is spread across the population. The aim of this article is to consider the economics of user charging and, in particular, what the introduction of charges might mean for the efficiency and equity of public service provision.

36 Thanks to Carol Propper, Carl Emmerson and Jessica Asato for useful comments on an earlier draft.

Some definitions – efficiency and equity

Before going any further, it is important to be clear about what is meant by efficiency and equity. Efficiency has two meanings. The first, sometimes called *allocative efficiency*, refers to whether the level of provision of a good or service is optimal from society's point of view – in economic terms, whether the marginal social benefit is equal to the marginal social cost. The second meaning, referred to as *technical* or *x-efficiency*, is about what quantity or quality of output can be derived from a given level of inputs. As discussed below, the introduction of user charging may affect both the allocative and x-efficiency of public service provision.

Equity (or fairness) also has a number of meanings. Horizontal equity demands the equal treatment of equals, although who is "equal" may be open to debate. Vertical equity, by contrast, is the unequal treatment of unequals (rich and poor) to achieve a "fairer" (typically a more redistributive) outcome. Notions of equity are much more value-laden than efficiency, making it hard to reach firm conclusions. Some people think that it is fair if people who benefit equally from a service are required to pay the same amount for it. Others think that those with an equal need for a public service should have equal access, but not necessarily pay equal amounts if they have very different levels of income. This paper will not make any judgements about whether or not user charging is fair, but will simply point to some relevant distributional considerations.

What is user charging?

User charging implies a particular model of delivering and financing public services[37] – i.e. the services are provided by the state and financed partly or wholly by the end user. Typically, user charging is contrasted with publicly-provided services financed out of taxation – and this will be the case here – but, as shown below, it is one of four possible models, including publicly-subsidised private provision. It is interesting that, in practice, it tends to be "social democratic"[38] countries such as Norway, Finland and Denmark, with a greater degree of public provision of services, which actually receive relatively more income from charges than "liberal" countries such as USA and UK with typically less public provision.[39]

Alternative models of public service provision

	Public provision	Private provision
Taxpayers pay	The welfare state	Subsidised provision
Individual users pay	User charges	The private sector

Implications for demand

Compared to a situation where public services are provided free and un-rationed at the point of delivery, the introduction of user charges will reduce individual consumption. As it was intended to do, the introduction of the congestion charge has reduced the number of people driving into London.

In the case of the congestion charge – as with other services that are over-consumed in the absence of any user-charge – the reduction in demand is likely to raise (allocative) efficiency. This is shown as Case 1 in Figure 1. Driving at peak times imposes costs on others – a negative externality in the form of an increase in congestion – that individuals do not directly bear (the social costs are higher than the private costs). Because individuals choose to drive up to the point where their benefit is equal to the private costs (i.e. they choose level Q'), the level of demand is too high from society's point of view (at Q' the social cost is greater than the benefit). The charge makes the social costs explicit and, in theory, demand will be reduced to its socially optimal level (Q*) assuming the charge is set at the right rate (C).[40]

40 An alternative to charging might be to ration demand in other ways (such as, in Athens, banning the use of cars with odd and even number plates on alternative days). However, charging is more efficient because it allows those who value road use the most to pay the charge and continue to drive.

Figure 1: User charges and allocative efficiency, un-rationed supply

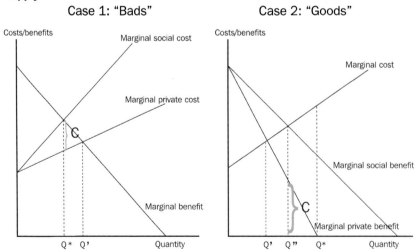

Typically, however, public services such as health and education are associated with positive externalities, i.e. the social benefits outweigh the private ones (Case 2 in Figure 1). If so, charging

41 See, for example, SMF (2003) *A fairer prescription for NHS charges*

individuals the full cost would result in under-consumption (Q') since individuals equate the cost with their private benefit, not the full social benefit. However, if the service is free and un-rationed, there may be excess demand (Q") such that the social benefits are less than the costs. In this case, charges can be used to fine tune the level of demand to bring social benefits and costs into line (Q*).

This is certainly true in theory, although achieving the optimum is complicated in practice by uncertainty over the magnitude of the social costs and benefits (where do the social cost/benefit curves lie in relation to the private cost/benefit curves?) and uncertainty over individual responsiveness to changes in price (what is the slope of the individual demand curve?).

Nevertheless, there are two points to take away from this simple analysis. One is that, in situations of excess demand, user charges can be used to achieve a more efficient level of public service provision. The other is that, in order to do this, user charges need to be flexible enough to accommodate varia-tions in marginal cost (in the case of different drugs, for exam-ple) and marginal private benefit (in the case of different higher education courses, for example). As has been argued elsewhere, a flat-rate prescription charge is likely to mean over-consump-tion of relatively more expensive drugs and under-consumption of cheaper ones.[41]

Distributional considerations

The distributional effects of moving from free and un-rationed supply to a situation of user charging are fairly obvious. The losers are those who previously enjoyed the service free at the point of use, while taxpayers are the winners (although of course they may also be consumers of the service). The intro-duction of user changes is likely to be unfair (vertical equity) if the service is typically consumed more by the less well off (healthcare); the reverse is true if it is typically consumed more by the better off (higher education, museums, driving into London). But, even in this latter case, user charging may be perceived as unfair (horizontal equity) if it reduces access to the service more among certain groups than others (and this was a large part of the opposition to charging for higher education).

Charging for healthcare is likely to be regressive compared to financing out of general taxation (vertical inequity) and may result in those with equal health needs not getting access to equal health care (horizontal inequity). Concern about vulnerable groups has meant exemptions from prescription charges for the elderly, children, pregnant women and those on low incomes, who together account for an estimated 85% of the value of prescriptions. In this case, the effect of such widespread exemptions is likely to attenuate the potential efficiency benefits, and financing out of general taxation may well be an easier solution, particularly given the cost of administering such exemptions.

Implications for supply

So far, user charging has been contrasted with free and un-rationed supply. But this is clearly an unrealistic counterfactual since almost all public services are rationed in some way. In a world of public service rationing, the relevant questions are, first, how rationing by willingness to pay (user charging) compares with other forms of rationing, and second, whether the introduction of charges can be used to expand supply.

In principle, user charging – rationing on the basis of willingness to pay – is likely to be economically more efficient than other forms of rationing since those who value the service more will be willing to pay for it (whether it is fair or not is a different matter). The exception is where consumers are unable to make well-informed decisions – most people don't know the value of many types of medical treatments, for example, and it may be better to let experts decide on the basis of medical need, or to ensure that consumers get the help they need to make informed choices (patient advisors were employed as part of the health choice pilot, for example).

As illustrated in Figure 2, the introduction of user charging can also be used to expand supply and, possibly, raise allocative efficiency.[42] If the service is free and un-rationed, consumers will demand Q" since at this point their marginal benefit is equal to the cost to them (zero). With limited funding for the service, however, supply is restricted to a maximum Q' and demand must be rationed, whether by waiting times (healthcare), qualifications (higher education) or some other means.

42 This analysis is taken from Robert Brent (1997) *Applied cost-benefit analysis*

43 This is because taxes may distort labour, consumption or investment choices.

44 In the case of the congestion charge, for example, nearly half of the £190m annual revenue is spent on administration.

With the introduction of user charges, available funding increases, depending on how willing consumers are to pay for the service, and, with extra revenue, supply can be expanded and the level of provision increased to Q^*. By coincidence, in this case, this is also the socially optimal level of service since the marginal social benefit is equated with the marginal cost.

Figure 2: User charges and allocative efficiency, supply rationed

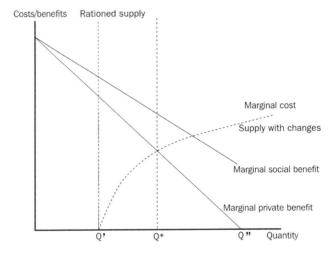

Why user charges and not general taxation?

If, as in Figure 2, the marginal social benefit is greater than marginal cost – and demand (private benefit) exceeds supply – an obvious question is why not raise more taxes to finance additional services. There are two possible answers – one is that taxes may impose a deadweight cost,[43] although there may also be a significant revenue cost in administering user charges.[44] The other is that there is public opposition to tax increases, as well as support for additional spending on specific services. These apparently irreconcilable public demands for lower taxes and higher spending have been seen as a contradiction – an example of people wanting to have their cake and eating it. But, there is a possible resolution – people may want to spend additional money on particular services, but they may not trust politicians to spend the tax revenue on the services they want. In this case, hypothecated taxes are seen by some as a potential solution to this problem.[45] If tax revenues are dedicated to particular services then politicians are constrained to spend money where the public wants it to go, public preferences over public spending are given greater voice and the public may be happier with a higher level of overall taxation. User charging may achieve similar ends – albeit with quite different distributional effects since people are required to vote with their wallets rather than with a ballot paper.

Of course, some of the objections to hypothecation apply equally to user charging. In particular, there is no guarantee that the introduction of user charges will increase total funding – the revenue from charges may simply substitute for existing tax revenue. But, if there is a credible way of ensuring that the revenue is additional to taxation, then user charging provides a potential mechanism for increasing overall spending on the services that the public wants.

Turning taxpayers into consumers

What about the effects of user charging on the x-efficiency of public services? As paying consumers, people may be more demanding than as taxpayers and have more of an incentive to shop around, and this may force the providers to cut costs or improve quality. But, to be effective as a mechanism for increasing x-efficiency, consumers need to have a degree of choice. User charging is likely to sharpen competitive pressure where consumers do have real alternatives, but, in the absence of choice, there is unlikely to be much real pressure on providers to improve quality or cut costs and a risk that consumers may become frustrated at having to pay for a service for which they have no real alternative.

Further distributional considerations

While those who were previously rationed will gain from the introduction of user charges and an increase in supply since they can now enjoy the service, those who previously enjoyed the service free at the point of use will lose. Since willingness to pay will to a large extent reflect ability to pay, the better off are more likely to be winners and the less well off will be relative

45 See, for example, Julian Le Grand (2003) *Motivation, agency and public policy: Of knights and knaves, pawns and queens.*

losers. Of course, it is possible to exempt vulnerable groups from user charges to make the overall system more equitable, but where the exempt groups constitute a big proportion of total consumers, this will severely limit the scope of user charging to raise additional funding, as well as being relatively expensive to administer. It would be hard to finance a new drug for the elderly or pregnant women by charging for it since they currently do not have to pay for prescriptions.

Core and periphery?

One possible way to reconcile efficiency and equity might be to use tax revenues to fund a basic core of services that are free to all, and to charge for supplementary services – this may be a wider set of services than are available in the core, or a higher quality (hotel-style facilities in a hospital, for example, or a shorter waiting time). This would allow an increase in the quantity/quality of public service provision, benefiting those who are willing to pay for it, while still providing a basic level of service for everyone, including the less well-off. The outcome would be not too dissimilar to the current situation where, faced with rationing in the public sector, those who can afford to, choose a higher quantity/quality of service provision from the private sector. So what are some of the arguments surrounding bringing a two-tier service inside the public sector?

One objection is a matter of principle – that the public sector should provide the same level of service for all, although rationally this is hard to reconcile with a situation where the better off use voice, choice and/or exit to get better services within the existing system. If the public sector can provide a better level (higher quality/lower cost) of supplementary services than the private sector, then allowing people to pay for those services via user charges has the potential to make at least some people better off, and no-one worse off (in economic terms, it is a pareto improvement). Those who currently opt out into the private sector are better off because they get access to better/cheaper supplementary services, those who can't afford to opt out into the private sector, but can afford to purchase supplementary services in the public sector are better off because they get access to supplementary services, while those who cannot buy the supplementary services are at least no worse off.[46] Of course, in all of this, the decision of which services are in and out of the core is clearly a crucial – and controversial – one.

But, there are a number of questions which need to be addressed:

Would user charging really mean more resources for the public sector, or could resources be diverted from providing core services for everyone to providing supplementary services for the better off? Tim Besley and Stephen Coate argue that if the better off opt out of the public sector this increases the resources available to the less well off.[47] If so, encouraging them back into the public sector with a higher quality/quantity of service may take resources away from the less well off.

Would providing supplementary services within the public sector strengthen or undermine levels of support for the welfare state? In a positive scenario, individuals who would otherwise go private are kept in the public sector and, as a typically fairly vocal constituency, actively support and even push to improve, the welfare state. In a rather more negative scenario, requiring people to pay directly for the services they use may result in increasing opposition to paying for others through taxation, undermining support for the welfare state. And, if supplementary public sector services are not better than the private sector alternative, the introduction of charges in the public sector may encourage more people to opt out into the private sector.

Conclusions

This article has briefly explored some of the efficiency and equity considerations of user charging. The main conclusions are:

*   Providing services free at the point of use and un-rationed may result in excess consumption; user charging can reduce demand to a more socially efficient level, but charges must be flexible and reflect underlying costs and benefits.
*   Where funding constraints mean limited supply and rationing of demand, the revenue from user charges can be used to increase supply, potentially benefiting those who would otherwise not enjoy the service.

---

46 This will not be the case for services with "positional externalities", such as higher education, where the value may depend on the relative quality of service. In this case, even if someone who cannot pay the supplement receives the same (absolute) quality of education as before they may be worse off (e.g. in the job market) if someone else can buy a higher quality of education.

---

47 Tim Besley and Stephen Coate (1991) "Public provision of private goods and the redistribution of income" *American Economic Review*

- User charging may also sharpen competitive pressure and result in efficiency improvements, but to be effective, there must be an element of choice.
- If the service is mainly consumed by the better off (e.g. higher education), user charging may be progressive compared to general taxation, but there may still be concern about equality of access.
- If the service is mainly consumed by the less well off, user charging will be regressive. Of course, vulnerable groups can be exempted, but this may be expensive to administer and reduce the benefits from user charging.
- Targeting user charging on supplementary services may help address equity concerns – although the definition of core and supplementary services is crucial, and likely to be controversial. Potentially, this may be a way of strengthening support for the welfare state by encouraging people to "go public" rather than private. But there is a risk that if people are forced to pay directly for services, they may be reluctant to pay again via taxation, and encouraged to go private. Understanding the links between paying for, using and supporting publicly-provided services is crucial.

User charging in public services: the case of tuition fees for higher education

Alissa Goodman,[48] **Institute for Fiscal Studies**

Introduction

Tuition fees provide a clear example of a 'user charge' in public services. Up until 1997, university tuition in England was provided free at the point of delivery for all those full-time domestic students who could gain a place. Fees were introduced for the first time in 1998, requiring non-exempted students to pay a flat fee of £1,000 p.a. Although this fee has been held constant in real terms since 1998 – with students currently paying £1,175 p.a. in academic year 2005/06 – this situation is about to change. The introduction of variable top-up fees in 2006/07 will mean that the maximum fee will rise to £3,000 per year, and that fees may be varied (subject to necessary "access" agreements) across courses and institutions.

Notably, this charging has been introduced with the aim of raising revenue for universities, in order to improve the quality of higher education (HE). However as with other user charges in the public services, it is also likely to have effects on people's behaviour, with consequences for the efficiency (in the broad economic sense) of the HE system. It is also likely to have important distributional consequences.

This paper assesses the changes in the funding regime currently underway, which are due to be fully in place by 2006/07. The paper argues that the reforms could in principle lead to a more efficient market for higher education, by more closely aligning the costs of a university degree to the benefits derived.

48 Thanks are due to Lorraine Dearden, Emla Fitzsimons, and Greg Kaplan at IFS. Thanks also to Nick Barr and Jessica Asato for their helpful comments on an earlier draft. Funding from the Nuffield Foundation, Grant number OPD/00294/G is gratefully acknowledged, as is co-funding from the ESRC Centre for the Microeconomic Analysis of Public Policy at IFS. All the usual disclaimers apply.

49 Department for Education and Skills, *2003, The Future of Higher Education*, Cm. 5735.

50 See for example L. Dearden, E. Fitzsimons and A. Goodman, 2004, *An Analysis of the Higher Education Reforms*, Briefing Note no. 45, London: Institute for Fiscal Studies (www.ifs.org.uk/bns/bn45.pdf) for a discussion of the evolution of the reforms. For overall assessments, see also L. Dearden, E. Fitzsimons, A. Goodman and G. Kaplan, 2005, *Higher Education Funding Policy: Who wins and who loses?* A comprehensive guide to the current debate, IFS Commentary No. 98, London: Institute for Fiscal Studies, (http://www.ifs.org.uk/comms/comm98.pdf), and N. Barr, 2004, Higher Education Funding, *Oxford Review of Economic Policy*, Vol. 20, No. 2, pp. 264-283.

Much concern has been expressed about the equity, or distributional consequences of the new top-up fee regime. This paper argues that some of the concerns about how the reforms will affect the incentive to attend university are probably misplaced, since the poorest students will be more than compensated for the increases in fees by large additions to up-front support in the form of maintenance grants and subsidies. Moreover, the extension of the current system of subsidised loans, with repayments linked to income will also make the funding more progressive than one funded fully from general taxation.

However, there will also be a significant group of potential students from lower-to-middle income families, for whom the cost of attending university will be increased. This is arguably one section of the population that the Government is trying to encourage to attend university. This suggests that the real concern should be about students from the lower-to-middle end of the parental income distribution, who could be adversely affected by the reforms.

The proposed reforms

The origin of the proposed reforms to higher education funding was the Department for Education and Skills' White Paper published in January 2003,[49] which set out plans for introducing top-up fees for higher education. The detailed evolution of the plans from their initial form into the Higher Education Act 2004, have been well-documented elsewhere.[50]

Under the new arrangements, maximum fees will be higher than their current level (though the minimum will be reduced, see below). In addition, there will be no exemptions for fees based on family income (see Table 1). Instead of being payable up front, all fees will be deferrable until after graduation, with loans available at a zero real interest rate, repayable according to income (at 9% above a threshold of £15,000). Fees will be variable, up to a £3,000 cap, which will remain in place at least until 2010. Students from the poorest backgrounds will receive new grants (up to £2,700) and bursaries (at least £300 for those paying the full fee). Further details, including changes to maintenance loans, are set out in Dearden et al, 2005 op cit.

Table 1. An outline of the pre-reform system and planned (or partially implemented) reforms[51]

The "pre-reform" system	The "new" system
Students would pay £1,200 in 2006/07 [52]	From 2006/07 students will pay £3,000
Up-front fee	Deferred fee (subsidised loans)
Flat fee rate	Variable fee rate
Exemptions based on family income	No exemptions
Pre-2004/05, no grant	Up to £2,700 in grants, plus additional bursaries

The balance between public and private contributions

As with other user charges, the introduction of top-up fees will shift the balance of funding between public and private contributions for tuition. Currently, the average total public and private contribution to tuition costs – amounting to around £6,000 per year – are skewed heavily towards the taxpayer (see Figure 1). Once fee exemptions are taken into account, only around £600, or around 10% is derived from the up-front fee, on average.

With the 2006/07 system in place, funding could increase by up to around 30%[53] on average in real terms per head, if all universities charged the full fee. This would return average funding per head to levels last seen in the early 1990s (but falling considerably short of the unit funding of £10,000 per year or more seen in the early 1970s). Under the new system, funding per head could rise to around £7,600, with the private fee contribution at around 38% of this. However a substantial proportion of the private fee revenue will still come from the public purse in the form of loan subsidies, which arise both because of the zero real interest rate to be charged on the new fee loans, and the provision for debt write-off after 25 years.[54] Taking into account the loan subsidy element of the fees, the private contribution will be around 22%.

As an illustration of how much further the balance could shift, the private contribution before taking into account loan subsidies would be around 50:50 if the fee cap were raised to £5,000 (which would be permitted from 2010). The net private contribution, after loan subsidies, would be at around 30% in this case.

51 Sources: Department for Education and Skills, *The Future of Higher Education*, Cm. 5735, 2003; *The Higher Education Bill*, Bill 35, 2004; *The Future of Higher Education and the Higher Education Act 2004: Regulatory Impact Assessment*, 2004; *Moving toward a Single Combined Grant for Higher Education*, 2004.

52 In 2005/06 the fee is £1,175, and in the absence of reform this is up-rated in line with inflation each year. For more detail, see Dearden et al 2005

53 This figure assumes that all universities charge the full fee, and that only the minimum bursary is paid out. Exactly how funding per head changes depends on the level of fees set and the actual bursaries universities decide to pay. The Office for Fair Access has estimated around 91% of HEIs and FECs are planning to charge the full tuition fee of £3,000, and that a 'typical' bursary would be considerably more than the minimum, at around £1,000. See Press Release from 17 March 2005 (www.offa.org.uk/news/2005/acc_agr.asp).

54 The DfES estimates that 42p of every £1 of fee loans will be paid for by the Exchequer due to the combination of these two elements of the loan subsidy. See Department for Education and Skills, 2004, *The Higher Education Act 2004: Regulatory Impact Assessment*.

55 Note: Public funding excluding loan subsidies is reduced between 2005-06 and 2006-07 due to removal of fee exemptions. The public money currently spent on fee exemptions will instead be channelled into grants. £5,000 fee cap calculations based on assumption that public funding per head remains constant if fee cap is lifted.

56 See for example, the submission from Universities UK to the 2004 Spending Review (http://bookshop.universitiesuk.ac.uk/downloads/SR2004.pdf)

Figure 1. The balance between public and private costs of tuition[55]

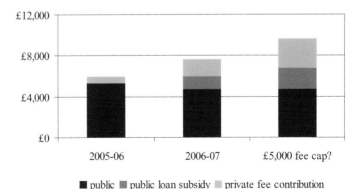

Source: Author's calculations based on Department for Education and Skills Departmental Report, 2005 Table 12.7 http://www.dfes.gov.uk/publications/deptreport2005/docs/2005deptrep.pdf, and National Statistics First Release SLC SFR 01/2004 Table 2C http://www.slc.co.uk/pdf/slcsfr012004.pdf. All figures up-rated to 2006-07 prices using GDP deflator.

More money for universities?

Clearly, universities will gain from the proposed reforms. As stated above, income per head could rise by up to 30% in real terms in 2006/07, a substantial jump reversing at least a decade of significant decline in funding per head. On aggregate, the university sector should gain in the region of £1.2 billion each year from the advent of top-up fees, making a significant inroad into the shortfalls the university sector has been keen to document.[56]

However raising money alone is not sufficient to make the case for extending a user charge in the public services. There would be many different ways of raising the same cash. This point is highlighted by the different approaches taken by the main political parties at the 2005 General Election campaign, each of which was designed to raise almost the same £1.2 billion additional funds per year for the university sector, but by different means. The Liberal Democrats promised to fund the entire increase through higher taxes (through increasing the higher rate of income tax for top earners), whilst the Conservatives planned to fund the boost to university revenues by scrapping the current generously subsidised maintenance loan regime, and gifting the outstanding value of the student loan book to the university sector. In both cases the plan was to raise this money whilst at the same time removing all tuition fees for domestic students.

Rather than relying on its revenue-raising properties, the economic case for top-up tuition fees[57] stands or falls on its other attributes, in particular whether the changes in incentives brought about are desirable either on efficiency or equity grounds. Ideally, these should be compared with the properties of the other alternatives for raising the same money. In Dearden et al, 2005a and 2005b, all three parties' policies are scrutinised in detail. Below we consider the likely efficiency and equity implications of the Government's plans.

57 I do not consider here any political case for raising fees, which might for example also take into account the relative "tax aversion" of the electorate and the "fee aversion" of potential graduates.

Do top-up fees improve economic efficiency?

In order to understand if top-up fees will improve economic efficiency, it is important to understand why the Government intervenes in the market for higher education in the first place. As well as reasons of distribution and fairness, which I turn to in the next section, there are a number of good reasons for government intervention, in order to make the HE market more efficient.

The primary reason is because of credit market failures. Since education is an investment, whose gains are primarily realised long after studying, a successful market for higher education requires a well-functioning credit market, allowing students to study when young and pay back later, and thereby make the optimal investment in their own education. Without the government there to help ensure this market works well, it is very likely that the private market would fail, and too few people would be able to go to university. The common problems of adverse selection, and moral hazard in the credit market, both of which arise from different forms of asymmetric information, are likely to be compounded in this context because of the lack of collateral available to most students, in order to back up their loans.

In addition to these credit market failures, there may also be positive externalities – or in other words, some social returns to investments in education, which individuals operating in a private market without any intervention would fail to take into account. Frequently cited externalities in the market for HE include both the benefits of a more cohesive society, and reductions in crime, as well as economic growth arising from innovation and technological gains. It is worth noting however

58 For more on the returns to Higher Education, see Blundell, R., Dearden, L. and Sianesi, B. (2004), 'Measuring the returns to education', in S. Machin and A. Vignoles (eds), *The Economics of Education in the UK*, Princeton University Press.

59 This estimate is based on an average male graduate total lifetime earnings of around £1 million, and graduate female lifetime earnings of £0.75m – see Dearden et al, 2005 op cit

60 For some evidence on this, see Chevalier, A., and Conlon, G. 2003 "Does it pay to attend a prestigious university?" Centre for the Economics of Education Discussion Paper No. 33 (http://cee.lse.ac.uk/cee%20dp s/ceedp33.pdf)

that the measurement of these social returns is controversial and they remain largely un-quantified.

Despite the clear case for government intervention, these reasons for intervention do not in themselves justify a 100% taxpayer subsidy, particularly in the context of the very large private returns deriving from HE (indeed in some countries, notably the US, the HE sector operates with far less intervention). Recent work undertaken at IFS suggests that a woman receives, on average, somewhere between 25% and 27% higher earnings as a result of undertaking higher education. The corresponding return for men is somewhere between 18% and 21%.[58] Over a lifetime, this average mark-up could amount to a total of around £200,000,[59] a large sum relative to the proposed fees of around £9,000 for a three year degree. However it is important to take into account other costs of university besides tuition, including foregone earnings during study, and to discount the flow of earnings over time, in order to make a more meaningful comparison of the mark-up. It is also the case that the financial returns to different degrees will vary quite markedly.[60]

These arguments suggest that some further extension of user charging for university education is likely to be justified on efficiency grounds. This is both because a higher maximum fee level seems justified given the potentially large private returns to higher education. At the same time, fee variability could in principle mean that the costs and benefits for different degree courses, which vary quite widely, could be more closely aligned.

A successful market for higher education requires a well-functioning credit market, allowing students to study when young and pay back later, and thereby make the optimal investment in their own education.

Fee variability might also allow some price competition within the university sector, thereby improving efficiency. However, the theoretical efficiency gains from introducing fee variability are unlikely to be realised in practice with the current fee 'cap' of £3,000, since almost all universities have stated that they will charge the full fee for all courses.

Some critics have pointed out the apparent inconsistency of this aim with the Government's stated ambition of increasing the number of young people going to university, since the increase in fees will effectively improve efficiency by curtailing excess demand, if university degrees are currently priced below their optimal level. However it is important to remember that the changes to fees are being put into place together with quite drastic changes to the system of up-front student support, and it is only by considering these together that the changes in incentives arising from the reforms can be fully understood.[61] This is discussed in more detail in the section below, which looks at the equity implications of the reforms.

What are the effects of top-up fees and other reforms to student support for the net costs of attending university, for students across the parental income scale?

Much concern has been expressed about the equity, or distributional consequences of the new top-up fee regime. Some of the concerns about how the reforms will affect the incentive to attend university, however, are misplaced, since the poorest students will be more than compensated for the increases in fees by large additions to up-front support in the form of maintenance grants and subsidies. On the other hand for all but the poorest students – specifically, those with joint parental income above around £19,500 per year – the incentive to attend university may actually be reduced. This is because the total additional costs of entering university under the new regime will outweigh the total additional payments made to them through the student support system.[62] Although this needs to be balanced against the fact that the removal of up-front tuition fees might remove some of their immediate liquidity constraints, it does suggest that perhaps the real concern should be about the effects of the reforms on students from the lower-to-middle end of the income distribution.

61 It is also important to consider the impact on incentives of the potential changes in Higher Education quality arising from the reforms. We do not, however, consider these here, see footnote 57, and Conclusions.

62 In this analysis I do not consider the changes in quality that might arise from the increased funding for universities. This means that I do not consider the potential improvement in education quality arising from the introduction of top-up fees as an additional benefit that students take into account when making their education decisions. However if the reforms lead to an increase in funding per head then this should, all other things being equal, increase both quality and, thereby, demand (i.e. improve the incentive to attend).

63 Given the zero real interest rate it makes sense for all students to borrow the maximum available to them.

64 Based on DfES projections, the average maintenance loan subsidy will be 29%, and the average fee loan subsidy will be 42%. If lifetime earnings are lower than the level that attracts the average loan subsidy, then the subsidy will be higher.

65 Note illustration is for student in first or second year living away from home outside of London. Source: Author's calculations. See Table 2 for selected calculations by family income.

The net financial improvement per year to a student from switching from the pre-reform system (which was the system in place in 2003/04) to entering under the new system (which will be in place in 2006/07) is illustrated in Figure 2. The calculations underlying this figure assume that a student takes out the maximum student loans,[63] receives the average loan subsidy through the course of their working life,[64] and incurs the maximum fee. To provide a better idea of how the calculations were derived, Table 2 shows the underlying calculations for a student on family incomes of less than £15,970, £24,000 and more than £44,000.

Clearly the effects vary considerably across the parental income distribution. Despite the higher fees and loss of fee remissions, the poorest students with family incomes below £15,970 should be more than £1,000 p.a. better off under the new system. This is because they will gain in grants, bursaries, and loan subsidies by £1,000 more than the additional fees they will be required to pay. If they go on to be low earners later in life, the advantage under the new system will increase.

Figure 2. The change in net financial position due to moving to the new funding regime (by parental income)[65]

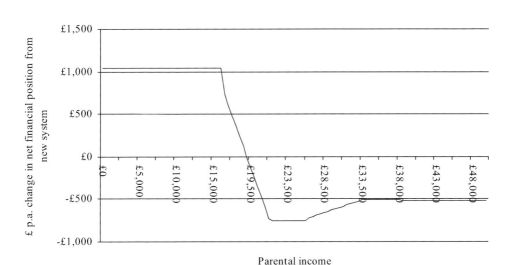

Parental income

However these benefits decline sharply with parental income, as the maintenance grant, bursary and maintenance loans are tapered away. For all those with family income above around £19,500 per year, the additional costs to entering HE out-weighs any additional benefits in the form of direct financial support from the state. Because of the way that the maintenance loan and grant tapers will operate, those paying the highest penalty for entering HE under the 2006/07 compared to the pre-reform system are those whose parents are on incomes between £22,100 and £26,000. It will cost these young people approximately £750 per year more in total to go to university.[66] It should be noted that this is a particularly dense part of the income scale and, depending on their exact family circum-stances, one with living standards that would place them largely in the 2nd and 3rd income deciles of the overall income distrib-ution. Arguably it is exactly students from these families that the Government is trying to encourage rather than to dissuade from attending university.

An additional imperative clear from this analysis is the importance of providing adequate financial information about the likely costs and benefits to all potential students.

66 Despite this deterioration in their net position, the removal of up-front tuition fees could reduce some immediate liquidity con-straints, as noted above.

Table 2. The change in net financial position due to moving to the new funding regime by parental income

	Family income £ p.a.		
	<£15,970	£24,000	>£44,000
Pre-reform system			
Costs of attending:			
Fees	1200	1200	1200
Payments for attending:			
Fee Remissions	1200	1043	0
Maintenance loan subsidy	1247	1247	935
Net position	**1247**	**1090**	**-265**
Post-reform system			
Costs of attending:			
Fees	3000	3000	3000
Payments for attending:			
Grant	2700	1043	0
Bursary	300	0	0
Maintenance loan subsidy	1031	1031	958
Fee loan subsidy	1260	1260	1260
Net position	**2291**	**334**	**-782**
Overall gain from switching systems (£ p.a.)	*£1,044*	*-£756*	*-£517*

67 However alternatives such as the Liberal Democrats' proposals to raise the revenue from those on incomes of £100,000 or more would be yet more concentrated amongst higher income households than the Government's plans.

What are the effects of top-up fee repayments on the distribution of income?

Another aspect of the 'equity' or 'fairness' of the proposed reforms is how the profile of those who will pay for the additional university funding compares to other alternatives, such as using tax increases to boost university incomes. Raising additional funding for universities through deferred fees is clearly more 'progressive' than raising the equivalent funding through general direct or indirect taxation, since most graduates end up well into the top half of the income distribution, whilst taxpayers are drawn from across the income scale.

As a simple illustration of this point, Figure 3 shows an estimate of the proportion of the total income of each decile group that would be required to raise an additional £1.2 billion from direct taxation, indirect taxation, and from the new Graduate Contribution Scheme (GCS), through which graduates will repay their fee loans.

In each case the percentages of total income required have been estimated using some simplistic assumptions. For example the direct and indirect tax (and combined direct + indirect) proportions are calculated assuming that the current burden of taxation is simply scaled up, to achieve the additional revenue. However it would be difficult to design any actual reforms to achieve this effect. The distribution of fee repayments has been estimated using the IFS tax and benefit model, with some rough rules of thumb for estimating which graduate households would be in repayment of their loans (loan repayments are then fixed at 9% if income is above a threshold of £15,000). For this reason figures should be taken as indicative only. They do show, however that the burden of repayments would fall much more heavily on lower income households if funded from general direct or indirect taxation compared to the new graduate repayment scheme.[67]

Figure 3. Illustrative pattern of payments across the income scale to raise £1.2 billion for universities

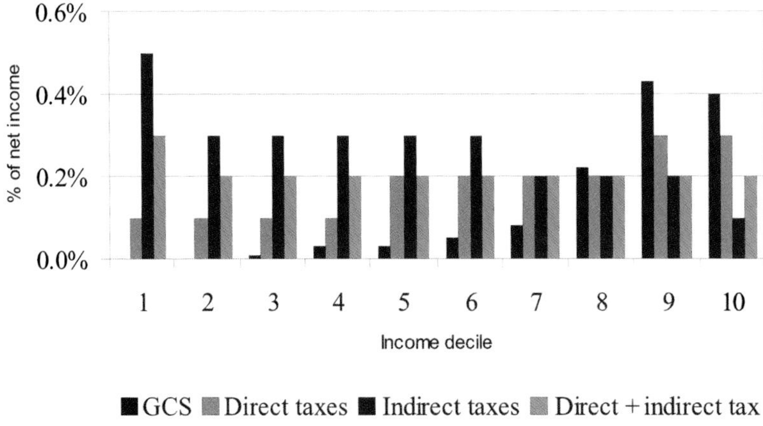

Source: direct and indirect taxation figures from ONS, 2004. GCS figures based on IFS calculations using IFS Tax and Benefit model (assumptions available from the author).

Conclusions

In conclusion, it is clear that the introduction of top-up fees will raise new money for universities. However such gains in revenue could be achieved in a number of different ways, as highlighted by the alternative proposals from the different political parties at the 2005 General Election. It is therefore vital to assess the case for extended user charging in this sector on a wider set of criteria, including its implications for efficiency and equity.

As discussed, new top-up fees could arguably improve efficiency in the sector, by more closely aligning the costs of attending university with the full, social benefits. This is because there are large private returns to attending university that are unlikely to call for 100% subsidy.[68] However making this argument for extended user charging implies that there is, under the current system, some level of excess demand that needs to be reduced. At first glance this appears incompatible with the Government's other aim, to increase the proportion of young people who attend higher education.

However these aims are perhaps not as incompatible as they at first seem. First, the resulting improvements in the

68 There might also be payoffs from the introduction of more competition within the university sector, as discussed earlier.

quality of HE arising from a better-resourced sector might mean that participation is not reduced despite the higher cost.

Second, it is important to take into account the other reforms to student support that are being put in place at the same time as the changes to tuition fees. As has been shown, although it is not young people from the lowest income backgrounds who will face any additional costs (indeed new grants and bursaries should make attending university more attractive for the very poorest), those from the low-to-middle part of the income distribution will be particularly hardest hit. Unless the benefits to the increased quality of education they might receive (due to a better-resourced university sector) are sufficiently attractive, it appears that the incentive for young people from these backgrounds to enter university will be reduced.

However, as has been shown, the equity implications of the reforms are complex and do not all point in the same direction. For example, despite these concerns about students from low-to-middle income backgrounds, the repayment system embodied in the top-up fee regime will almost certainly be more progressive than raising the same money through general taxation.

User charges for health care: history and prospects

Peter C. Smith, Centre for Health Economics, University of York

Introduction

Most health care is directed at individual patients, seeking to improve the duration and quality of life. It is therefore perfectly feasible to charge patients a fee for their use of health care. Indeed it is worth recalling that until recently doctors in all countries relied mainly on patient fees to provide their income. It was only in the latter half of the twentieth century that socialised medical care became widespread in developed countries.

User charges in health care have two broad roles: to raise finance for the health system, and to send signals to patients who would otherwise face a zero price for access to health care. Developed countries do not rely to any great extent on charges as a significant source of finance. However, there has been a persistent concern with the dangers of 'moral hazard' in health care.[69] That is, in the absence of direct prices, patients may use health care when it is not warranted. Moreover, given the power of doctors to influence patient behaviour, moral hazard might be exacerbated by 'supplier induced demand', particularly in systems where doctors' incomes rely directly on attracting high levels of business.[70]

This paper first examines the extent to which OECD countries currently rely on user charges in health care. It then describes some recent European policy innovations, and outlines some important findings from the RAND experiment with variable levels of user charge in the US. The paper ends with some comments on the role of user charges in the future.

69 Zweifel, P. and Manning, W. (2000), "Moral hazard and consumer incentives in health care", in J. P. Newhouse and A. J. Culyer (ed), *Handbook of health economics*, Amsterdam: Elsevier.

70 McGuire, T. (2000), "Physician agency", in J. P. Newhouse and A. J. Culyer (ed), *Handbook of health economics*, Amsterdam: Elsevier.

User charges in high income countries

Early experiments with subsidised health care in countries such as Germany and Britain were aimed predominantly at improving the health of low income workers and the military. These evolved gradually into the systems of universal health insurance coverage and low user charges are now in place in most OECD countries. Figure 1 shows the current pattern of private health care financing in OECD countries, underlining the heavy reliance on public funds, in the form of tax or social insurance revenues.

Direct user charges (out of pocket payments) account for between 10% and 20% of revenue. Most of the 'other' private expenditure relates to voluntary private insurance. In particular, in countries such as France and Ireland, patients are in principle liable for quite high user charges. However, many citizens take out voluntary private health insurance to secure protection from out of pocket payments. Note that the OECD has not been able to report these data for the UK since 1997.

Figure 1: Private expenditure as % total health expenditure 2001

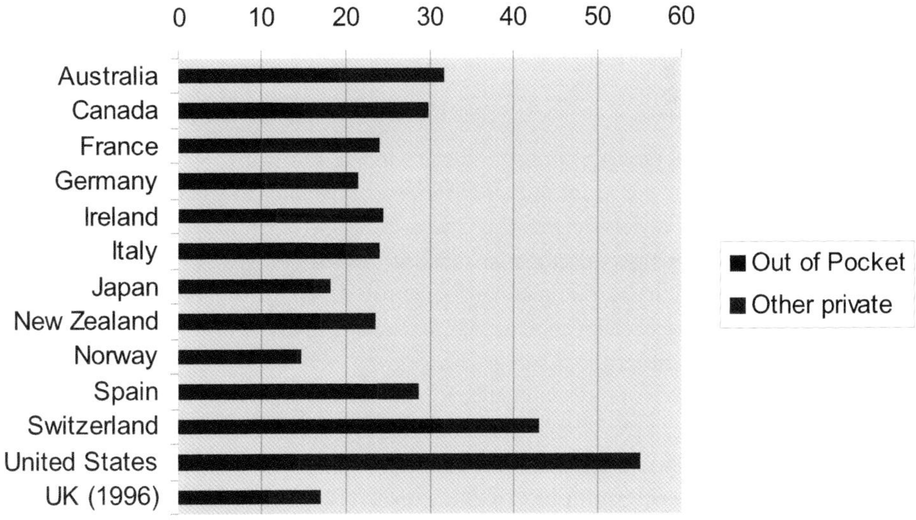

(Source: OECD Health Data 2004)

Figure 2 shows trends in the use of out-of-pocket payments, as a percentage of total health expenditure. Although there is no discernible trend in this proportion, the absolute value of direct patient payments for health care has generally increased over the period, because health care expenditure in total has increased sharply in most countries as a proportion of the total economy.

71 Eversley, J. (2001), "The History of NHS Charges", *Contemporary British History*, 15(2), 53-75.

72 House of Commons (2005), *Hansard 27 Jan 2005 : Column 561W*, London: The Stationery Office.

Figure 2: Trends in out-of-pocket payments as % total health expenditure

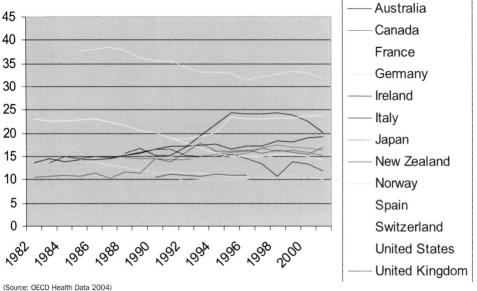

(Source: OECD Health Data 2004)

The especially low reliance on user charges in the United Kingdom reflects the founding principle of a NHS 'free at the point of access'. Eversley relates the fraught history of NHS charges, the imposition of which in 1951 led to the resignation of Aneurin Bevan, hastening the demise of the Attlee Government.[71] An attempt to abandon prescription charges by the Labour Government in 1965 was soon reversed in 1967, and further increases were subsequently imposed in 1975 under pressure from the International Monetary Fund. In 2004 prescription charges in England accounted for income of £446 million, with only 8.9% of prescriptions directly attracting the full charge of £6.20.[72] The vast majority of prescriptions are exempt from charges on grounds of age (young and older people),

73 Robinson, R. (2002), "User charges for health care", in E. Mossialos, A. Dixon, J. Figueras and J. Kutzin (ed), *Funding health care: options for Europe*, Buckingham: Open University Press.

sickness (certain chronic conditions), maternity, or low income. The Welsh Government intends to abolish prescription charges by 2007, and the Scottish Parliament is currently considering their abandonment.

It is also worth noting that many lower income countries do not offer patients the protection from charges enjoyed in high income countries. Indeed, worldwide over 50% of health care finance is in the form of out of pocket payments. High reliance on user charges is inescapable in low income countries in which a governmental or private insurance capacity is infeasible, and generally leads to poor health system performance. It is therefore important to emphasize that the discussion in this paper is relevant only for developed health systems.

Recent developments in Europe

Western European countries have traditionally sought to model their health systems on the principle of 'solidarity'. This implies universal coverage, and contributions to the financing of health care according to ability to pay, irrespective of age or level of sickness. User charges appear to contradict the principle of solidarity. Yet, as expenditure on health care has grown inexorably, there has been growing interest in imposing some modest charges.[73]

In general, these new charges do not raise a significant volume of finance for the health system – indeed in some circumstances the sums involved are outweighed by the collection costs. Rather, the main purpose of these experiments is to encourage patients to use the health system to better purpose, by discouraging treatment when benefits are small and incentivising efficient use of services when it is justified. Examples of objectives underlying charging schemes include:

* moderating use of drugs
* encouraging use of cheaper generic drugs
* discouraging multiple consultations of alternative doctors
* directing patients through gatekeeper physicians
* encouraging the use of less costly or higher quality 'preferred' providers
* encouraging early discharge of patients from hospital.

Most of these initiatives have been directed at cost containment, and many other experiments in a similar vein could be envisaged, such as charging patients for outpatient visits, but offering a full or partial rebate if the first appointment is honoured (in order to discourage 'did not attends'). Moreover, user charges could in principle be used to encourage healthier behaviour on the part of patients. For example, one could envisage a scheme of exemption from charges if a patient complies with a course of treatment in its entirety. There follows a brief sketch of a few recent European innovations.

Sweden

Sweden was one of the first of the traditional public sector systems to experiment with quite small user charges across a wide range of health services. Children and young people are generally exempt, and the maximum annual liability for charges has traditionally been set at quite a low level (90 in 2001). Charging on this modest scale appears to have been generally accepted as reasonable, but it has resulted in reduced utilisation amongst low income patients, and a concern that equity of access may be compromised.[74]

Netherlands

The Netherlands relies on a system of competitive social insurance, and has traditionally repudiated use of direct charges. However, from 2005 insurers have been allowed to offer premium discounts to insurees who make no use of hospital inpatient facilities in the preceding year, in effect imposing a charge for hospital use.

Germany

From 2004 Germany has experimented with a €10 charge for the first appointment with a doctor in each three month period, up to an income-related maximum. Initial findings suggest little change in the proportion of patients making some contact with a doctor, but some reduction in the average number of contacts made. There is no evidence of a disproportionate impact on the poor or sick, so an early evaluation is therefore cautiously optimistic that the reform is reducing intensity of use without harming patients.[75]

74 Andersen, R., Smedby, B. and Vågeröc, D. (2001), "Cost containment, solidarity and cautious experimentation: Swedish dilemmas", *Social Science & Medicine*, 52(8), 1195-1204.

75 Gericke, C., Wismar, M. and Busse, R. (2003), *Cost-sharing in the German health care system. Discussion Paper*, Berlin: Department of Health Care Management, Technische Universität Berlin. Grabka, M., Schreyögg, J. and Busse, R. (2005), *Verhaltensänderung durch Einführung der Praxisgebühr und Ursachenforschung - eine empirische Analyse. DIW Discussion Paper 506*, Berlin: Deutsches Institut für Wirtschaftsforschung.

76 Bellanger, M. and Mossé, P. (2005), "The search for the Holy Grail: combining decentralised planning and contracting mechanisms in the French health care system", *Health Economics*, forthcoming.

77 Kanavos, P. and Reinhardt, U. (2003), "Reference Pricing For Drugs: Is It Compatible With U.S. Health Care?" *Health Affairs*, 22(3), 16-30.

78 Lewis, M. (2002), "Informal health payments in central and eastern Europe and the former Soviet Union: issues, trends and policy implications", in E. Mossialos, A. Dixon, J. Figueras and J. Kutzin (ed), *Funding health care: options for Europe*, Buckingham: Open University Press.

France

In France, from January 2005 patients have been charged a small fee (€1) for each consultation, intervention and test. Also, for adults not suffering a long term illness, a supplemental charge is made for consulting a specialist without the endorsement of a nominated 'gatekeeper' physician (medicin traitant). This charge is variable, but for a basic consultation it is about €7. French patients have traditionally enjoyed unfettered access to health care professionals, so this is a tentative attempt at moderating demand for specialist care. In order that it can have the intended effect, policy makers are seeking to prevent inclusion of the new charges in the traditional complementary insurance used by many French citizens.[76]

Reference prices

A form of user charge that is widespread within Europe arises from the use of 'reference prices' for drugs (examples include Sweden, Germany, Spain and Italy). Under this regime, pharmaceuticals with similar properties are grouped into discrete 'clusters'. Patients are reimbursed at a fixed rate for all drugs within a cluster, and if they choose a more expensive drug they must pay the difference between the drug price and the reference price out of their own pocket. The intention is to encourage use of cheaper generic replacements of branded drugs.[77] The impact of reference pricing on demand and health outcomes has yet to be satisfactorily evaluated.

Slovak Republic

Some countries in eastern Europe are experiencing especially severe problems with financing health care, and are therefore experimenting with more radical approaches to charging, especially where a tradition of 'informal' payments to doctors and other professionals exists.[78] A particularly ambitious scheme of 'diagnosis based reimbursement' is being introduced in the Slovak republic. A national tariff for reimbursing providers is set for all interventions, according to diagnosis. Patients will then be reimbursed for a proportion of the costs of treatment, depending on the diagnosis group. The proportion reimbursed depends on the estimated benefits and costs of treatment, and there is full reimbursement for 33% of diagnoses.

This scheme is consistent with the prescriptions of the economic theory of 'optimal' commodity taxation.[79] However, as experience unfolds, it will be important to see whether it is in practice sustainable, whether unintended behavioural responses on the part of doctors or patients emerge, and whether the lack of exemptions leads to especially adverse outcomes for poor and sick people.

Evaluating user charge experiments

There is in general a shortage of reliable evidence on the impact of user charges on the utilisation of health care and the health of patients in developed countries. The major exception is the celebrated RAND experiment, under which over 2,000 US patients were randomly assigned to one of four charging regimes over an extended period.[80] One group of patients enjoyed complete freedom from charges, while those at the other extreme were charged 95% of fees for virtually all care, up to a maximum annual 'catastrophic' liability of about $6,000 at current prices.

Some results from the experiment are summarized in Table 1. They show consistent reductions in utilisation across all types of health care as the charges became more severe. For example, physician consultations varied from 4.55 per annum amongst those incurring no charges, to 2.73 amongst those in the highest charging scheme, a reduction of 40%. However, with one major exception, evaluation of the experiment did not detect any material variations in health outcome associated with charging. Researchers have therefore concluded that – for most of the population – charges succeeded in encouraging less profligate use of health care without serious health consequences.

79 Smith, P. (2005), "User charges and priority setting in health care: balancing equity and efficiency", *Journal of Health Economics*, 24, 1018-1029.

80 Newhouse, J. (1993), *Free for all? Lessons from the RAND health insurance experiment*, Cambridge MA: Harvard University Press.

Results from Belgium suggest a distinct impact of charges on demand for GP home visits and office visits, except amongst older or disabled patients.

Table 1: Use and spending per person in the RAND health insurance experiment

	Visit rates		Admission rates		Spending (2003$)	
Coinsurance (percent)	Number	SE	Number	SE	Amount	SE
0 (free care)	4.55	0.17	0.128	0.0070	1,377	58
25	3.33	0.19	0.105	0.0070	1,116	51
50	3.03	0.22	0.092	0.0166	1,032	58
95 (high deductible)	2.73	0.18	0.099	0.0078	946	47

Source: Newhouse, 2004

81 Newhouse, J. P. (2004), "Consumer-Directed Health Plans And The RAND Health Insurance Experiment", *Health Affairs*, 23(6), 107-113.

82 Van De Voorde, C., Van Doorslaer, E. and Schokkaert, E. (2001), "Effects of cost sharing on physician utilisation under favourable conditions for supplier-induced demand", *Health Economics*, 10(5), 457-471.

The one important exception was the finding that charging had a seriously adverse effect on those who were both poor and suffering from poor health. The RAND evaluation estimated that for this disadvantaged group there were a wide range of serious consequences, in spite of some cost subsidy for low-income families. For example, when charges were imposed, hypertension was less well controlled in this group, to the extent that the annual likelihood of death rose approximately 10%.[81]

It has proved much more difficult to evaluate the consequences of user charges where there is no experimental design, and researchers have had to resort to econometric analysis to infer their impact. However, when analysis has been undertaken in other countries, it appears to corroborate the RAND results. For example, results from Belgium suggest a distinct impact of charges on demand for GP home visits and office visits, except amongst older or disabled patients.[82]

Concluding comments
In the light of the above discussion, the question arises: what is the most appropriate role for user charges in a modern health system? Experience in high income countries suggests a persistent tension between the equity goal of assuring universal access to health care and the efficiency goal of assuring frugal use of health services. In short, unless carefully designed, user charges designed to curb excessive demand amongst the bulk of the population could have ruinous financial or health conse-

quences for a relatively small number of poor people with
health problems. It is therefore important to view the design
of user charges within the broader objectives and institutions
of the health system as a whole.

83 Coulter, A. and Ham, C.
(2000), *The Global Challenge
of Health Care Rationing*,
Maidenhead: Open University
Press.

With the notable exception of the United States, there is
a general consensus that public funding of tightly regulated
delivery should lie at the core of the modern health system.
However, there is also a growing trend in such systems towards
the use of small but symbolically important user charges.
Why this should be the case may be a matter for psychologists,
sociologists and political scientists to explain, as – from an
economic perspective – they appear insufficient to affect
demand materially, except amongst the very poor, who are
often exempt. Rather, the intention of new charging initiatives
seems to be to influence very specific aspects of patient
behaviour, and to act as a signal of preferred behaviour. In
this respect, in conjunction with a system of carefully crafted
exemptions, they may offer an important policy option for
influencing demand. Moreover, they may help reassure the
taxpayer that patients are being encouraged to use the
services they pay for responsibly.

However, notwithstanding the modest nature of these
recent developments, I believe that in the medium term the
accelerating pace of technological innovation and the inexorable
rise in patient demands may require a more fundamental
rethink of the use of charges. At present, European countries
are (just about) able to ensure that most mainstream interventions
are included in their statutory package, allowing policy makers
to claim that coverage is comprehensive. However, there is
growing evidence that such a policy may become financially
unsustainable, and that policy may have to resort to increased
use of explicit rationing of health care.[83]

If it does, the central policy problem is to decide which
health care technologies should be subsidised from public
funds. User charges policy then flows naturally from the choice
of the subsidised treatments. Once the 'public' package of care
is chosen, patients would still be free to purchase the remaining
unsubsidised interventions at market prices, or to purchase
complementary private insurance to cover such interventions.
This is the essence of the Slovak experiment. I have shown

84 Smith, P. (2005), *The statutory health care package under private health insurance*. Paper presented to World Bank conference on Voluntary Health Insurance in Developing Countries, Wharton Business School, University of Pennsylvania.

85 De Graeve, D. and Van Ourti, T. (2003), "The distributional impact of health financing in Europe: a review", *The World Economy*, 26(10), 1459-1479.

elsewhere that, from an economic perspective, the choice of interventions in the public package should be guided solely by the expected health benefits they bestow in relation to costs.[84] Equity concerns should in my view be tackled not by the health care system, but by the tax system used to finance the public package. However, if political considerations demand that the package should be skewed in favour of diseases of the poor, then this does not affect the general principle of explicit definition of the package.

The scope of the statutory package will be determined by the public's willingness to pay the necessary taxes – in particular, the willingness of the healthy and the rich to subsidise the sick and the poor.[85] It is therefore essential that the package is of high quality, so that richer people do not choose to use private care in preference to publicly subsidised care. If quality is poor, widespread resistance to paying the taxes required to finance the public package may arise, making the public system unsustainable.

In England, the National Institute for Health and Clinical Excellence (NICE) is charged with evaluating new technologies, and issuing associated clinical guidelines. Therefore, although a daunting technical undertaking, NICE could in principle be given the expanded remit of recommending the entire scope of the publicly subsidised package. Charges (partial or total) would then be paid by patients on interventions that fell outside the chosen package. Indeed one could envisage that – if a technology fails its cost-effectiveness criterion – NICE could nevertheless determine the (lower) price at which the intervention or drug could be included in the public package. The patient would then be asked to fund the difference between the NICE price and the provider's price.

Whether charges are symbolic or substantive, the issue of exemptions has proved problematic for policy makers. For example, successive UK governments have introduced exemptions for prescription charges on the grounds of age (young and old), health needs (an apparently arbitrary selection of conditions) and income, resulting in a very low proportion of patients being liable for charges. Clearly exemptions can often be arbitrary and pervert the intended economic signals. Yet equally, the evidence from RAND and other experiments is that at least some disadvantaged patients will suffer catastrophic financial or health effects if some system of abatement of charges is not put in place.

In summary, therefore, I believe that the publicly funded health system of the future should look something like the following:

- an explicit set of interventions is subsidised by public funds (the 'health basket'), the choice of which is guided by the criterion of cost-effectiveness;
- the size of the health basket is determined by the willingness of the population to pay the necessary taxes;
- charges (partial or total) are paid by patients on interventions that are not deemed cost-effective;
- those able and willing may purchase voluntary (complementary) insurance to protect against such charges;
- there should be no compromise on the quality of publicly funded health care, the intention being that all citizens should use the public sector for interventions within the health basket;
- there may be small charges even on fully subsidised interventions, as signals of preferred behaviour – these cannot be insured in the private market;
- there may need to be a carefully crafted system of exemptions from charges to protect very poor citizens.

This system may at first glance appear unattractive compared to the stated principle of a comprehensive NHS, free at the point of access. Yet many commentators feel that it will be infeasible to adhere to that principle indefinitely, as the scope of health care increases inexorably and the limits to popular willingness to pay the necessary taxes are reached. If this is the case, the proposals set out here offer policy makers a framework for making the hard choices that follow. It will take political courage to implement such explicit rationing, but the alternative may be steadily to reduce the scope and quality of the NHS by stealth, and reduce the widespread support for tax funding of the NHS, an outcome that cannot be beneficial to the general public good.

Co-payments in UK local government

Stephen J. Bailey, Professor of Public Sector Economics, Glasgow Caledonian University

Introduction

The term 'co-payments' refers to the financing of services by both the state (via taxes) and service users (via charges). The difference between a tax and a charge is that the former is an unrequited payment whereas the latter payment is conditional upon receipt of service. In principle, assuming ability to pay, the balance of co-payments between the state and service user should reflect the balance between the wider benefits to society and the personal benefits to the individual.

Charges exist in a complex policy environment, one that involves important legal, political, social and financial factors. They can be inequitable, even iniquitous if they constrain access to services by low-income groups more than by higher-income groups. Nevertheless, they are a strategic instrument for the achievement of value for money and can be used to promote social justice and choice in facilitating access to service by socially excluded groups.

Charges, therefore, are not just a balancing item in local government accounts meant to raise revenue to fill the gap between expenditures and income from grants and council tax, or simply to curb demand. Charges serve many more functions. They can serve as a signal of demand. They are 'fair', in the sense that people who use the service are paying towards the cost of providing the benefit they receive. They are educative in informing members of the public as to the cost of public service provision.

The willingness of the general public to pay for more services on a variable 'pay-as-you-use' basis depends upon whether the Government changes the nature of the welfare state from cradle-to-grave 'take-it-or-leave-it' state paternalism to mutual responsibility based on a variable combination of collective and individual financing via co-payments. Service users will almost always prefer tax financing since they usually capture the bulk of benefits whilst costs are spread across the generality of taxpayers. Service practitioners may also prefer tax financing because it is more certain than income from charges and free services generally improve social welfare.

86 Local Government Finance: Report of the Committee of Enquiry (The Layfield Report) Cmnd 6453 1976 London: HMSO, p. 290.

History of local government charges

Charging policies historically have not been seriously developed, the potential of charging generally being neglected by central governments. In particular, charges have not figured significantly in past reforms of local government finance. Typically, councillors' briefing documents pay little or no attention to charges, even though there has long been a significant degree of discretionary authority for use of charges. This may be because there has been (and still is) no uniform national policy for use of local government charges. The result is that charges are developed on an ad hoc service-by-service basis, there very rarely being local corporate policies on service charges.

As long ago as 1976, the Layfield Committee on local government finance considered a substantially increased role for charges but recognised the profound implications for the welfare state. Nevertheless, it concluded that "there may well be scope for increasing the proportion of local government revenue derived from charges without any radical change in social policies."[86] This conclusion related to the then 'old Labour' social policies.

A decade after the Layfield Report, the Conservative Government's 1986 White Paper 'Paying for Local Government' concluded that "charging users for a local authority service is an even more direct way of ensuring that local people can see what they are getting for what they are paying. Charging has benefits in terms of efficiency as well as accountability. Where consumers have a choice whether to pay for a service or not, those who provide the service can accurately

87 *Paying for Local Government* Cmnd 9714 1986 London: HMSO, p. 53.

88 *Strong Local Leadership: Quality Public Services* Cm 5237 2001 Department of Transport, Local Government and the Regions London: The Stationery Office. *Funding the Scottish Parliament, National Assembly for Wales and Northern Ireland Assembly* 3rd Edition 2002 London: HM Treasury.

89 *Modernising Local Government Finance: A Green Paper* 2000 London: Department of the Environment, Transport and the Regions.

90 Quoted in White, M. and Wintour, P. 'Tony Blair Interview: New Routes to Social Justice' *The Guardian* 28th November 2003 p. 4.

judge the real level of demand. Realistic charging policies help to improve the efficient use of services."[87] Whilst equity was not being ignored, more attention was being paid to economy, efficiency and effectiveness (i.e. value for money). However, like the Layfield Report, the 1986 White Paper had little or no impact on policy regarding the use of charges.

Regional devolution has been in place since 1999 and revenues from fees and charges are not subject to regional resource equalisation.[88] This means that income from charges is not offset by reduced Westminster block grants to the UK territorial governments. Whilst it may be thought that this provides a financial incentive to use charges to generate additional income, territorial governments have been more prone to abolish high profile charges outside the local government sector. Most notably, the Scottish Parliament abolished up-front university tuition fees and charges for personal care for the elderly. Similarly the Welsh Assembly abolished prescription charges for 16-25 year olds and, like Scotland, has ruled out top-up fees for university students. The only devolved tier to make more use of charges is the Greater London Authority, having introduced road congestion charges in February 2003.

In 1998/99 only 11% of revenue funding came from sales, fees and charges, 22% came from local taxes, 22% from business rates and 45% from central government grant.[89] This led to claims that local authorities are too heavily dependent upon central government grants and, subsequently, to the establishment of the Balance of Funding Review. In its response to the Review, the Local Government Association suggested additional local taxes and granting councils powers to levy charges across more services, such as removal of graffiti, CCTV and home energy services. It recommended that the Review Group examine the scope for increasing income from charges across the generality of services.

During the UK Labour Government's 'Big Conversation', Prime Minister Tony Blair stated that "the big notion is the recasting of the 1945 welfare state, so that the values of that remain, but where we live in a world where the relationship between the citizen and the state is one of mutual responsibility, not one of paternalism."[90] Furthermore, "I passionately believe

… you can expand public services and protect quality but you can only do this in the modern world if people see a fair way of paying for these services. This is an argument that goes right to the heart of what the Government believes."[91]

Charges are seen as a means of promoting Best Value, explicit reference being made to this in the English Green Paper on local government finance,[92] reflecting all their functions noted above. Taxes are therefore being used to spend more on pre-school and school education (as well as the NHS) whilst charges are being used to increase spending on universities and roads, etc.

Legal authority governing the use of charges

The 1989 Local Government and Housing Act and other statutes disallow charges for core education services in schools, core library services, fire fighting, core police services and for electoral registration and the conduct of elections. The Local Government in Scotland Act 2003 is the same as the 1989 Local Government and Housing Act in this respect but leaves open the possibility of charging for other forms of education (except relating to public libraries), training and fire safety advice provided by the fire service, use of vacant spaces on school buses and 'reasonable' charges for new services under the 'power of well-being'.

The Local Government Act 2003 contains a general power for the 552 'best value authorities' in England and Wales to charge for discretionary services provided under the well-being powers in the Local Government Act 2000. Local authorities must already have the power to provide the service if they are to make use of the new charging powers under the Local Government Act 2003. Use of the charging power is discretionary and individual authorities may, if they wish, provide discretionary services free of charge and different people can be charged different amounts, discounts being allowed for prioritised groups. These new powers do not override any other legislation prohibiting charges. Income from charges must not exceed the costs of provision (perhaps calculated with reference to the CIPFA definition of total cost in its Best Value Accounting Code of Practice), over a reasonable period of time (between, say, one and three years). Moreover, the recipient

91 Quoted in Toynbee, P. 'Foolish and Dangerous: Blair's tuition fees package is a fair one, but his determination to charge for public services should be resisted' *The Guardian* 16 January 2004 p.27.

92 *Modernising Local Government Finance: A Green Paper* 2000 London: Department of the Environment, Transport and the Regions.

93 General Power for Best Value Authorities to Charge for Discretionary Services – Guidance on the Power in the Local Government Act 2003 London: Office of the Deputy Prime Minister, paras. 10 and 15. [www.local.odpm.gov.uk/guidprop.pdf]

94 Ibid. para. 11, and General Power for Best Value Authorities in Wales to Charge for Discretionary Services – Guidance on the Power in the Local Government Act 2003 Cardiff: National Assembly for Wales, para. 11. [www.wales.gov.uk]

of the discretionary service must have agreed to its provision and to pay for it via a charge.

The Government's aim is "to encourage authorities to provide more wide-ranging and new and innovative services for their communities… to provide those sorts of services they would otherwise decide not to provide (or improve) at all because they cannot justify or afford to provide them for free or to improve them. The aim is not to provide a new source of income for authorities, but to allow them to cover their costs."[93] Choice is facilitated without compromising access to public services because "services that an authority is mandated or has a duty to provide are not discretionary and will not benefit from the new power at section 93 of the 2003 Act. However, additions or enhancements to such mandatory services above the level or standard that an authority has a duty to provide may be discretionary services." [94]

The Local Government Act 2003 is potentially confusing because national minimum standards have not been established for most services. Hence, charges may be subject to legal challenge, in which case the courts may have to establish precisely what levels of services local authorities have a duty to provide. However, the 1976 Layfield Committee (op cit) concluded that establishing minimum standards would be highly problematic because of difficulties in defining them in output (or outcome) rather than input terms. Nevertheless, two notes of dissent in the Layfield report argued that central government should define minimum standards of output for local government services to clarify and strengthen financial accountability, not just between central and local government but also between the state and the individual, the latter paying charges for use of services above the minimum standards financed from taxation.

Charges are seen as a means of promoting Best Value, explicit reference being made to this in the English Green Paper on local government finance

----

The scope for charges in local government

Excluding housing rents, charges raised only £3 to £4 per head of population per week in 2003/04, little changed since the 1990s.[95] Charging systems are highly variable, involving a web of flat-rate charges, means-tested charges, concessions and exemptions from charges. The percentages of costs recovered through charges vary dramatically: parking and property enquiries make accounting profits, whereas library and police services only cover several percent or so of costs.[96] In general, educational, cultural and protective services cannot achieve high rates of cost recovery through charges.

The Institute for Public Policy Research has argued the future of charges lies in the extent to which they promote attainment of key social, environmental and economic objectives and are recognised as legitimate by their electorates.[97] The attainment of these three categories of objectives is an extension of value for money and Best Value, including economy, efficiency and effectiveness as well as equity. Charges are not likely to be acceptable to electorates if their sole or primary aim is simply to raise revenue. They may be more acceptable if they raise additional revenue used for service improvements.

The services for which greater use of charges may be made are those which experience increases in centrally prescribed charges or where there is increased local discretion to charge. There now follows a summary of options, further details being available elsewhere.[98] Council house rents are being raised in England in accordance with a central government formula to levels charged by housing associations.[99] Housing authorities could also levy new or higher service charges for communal cleaning and concierge services as well as for internal redecoration, home security services, energy advice, etc.

Centrally-prescribed planning fees are continuing to rise to recover a higher proportion of the costs of processing planning applications. Planning obligations negotiated between local authorities and developers and/or locally determined planning charges are expected to be of greater proportionate importance in the future. This might help to recover councils' infrastructure costs related to physical development, especially in fast-growing suburban municipalities and in South-East England.

Discretionary charges for city road use are currently

95 *The Challenge of Charging: A Managed Response*, Accounts Commission for Scotland 1998 Edinburgh. *The Price is Right? Charges for Council Services*, Audit Commission 1999 London: HMSO. Local Government Financial Statistics England 2004 Office of the Deputy Prime Minister London: HMSO. Scottish Local Government Financial Statistics 2004 Scottish Executive Edinburgh: HMSO.

96 CIPFA 2005 London: Chartered Institute of Public Finance and Accountancy. [www.cipfastats.net]

97 Robinson, P. (2004) *How Do We Pay? Funding Public Services in Europe* London: Institute for Public Policy Research. [www.ippr.org]

98 Bailey, S. J. (2005) *Local Government Charges* CIPFA Technical Information Services London: Chartered Institute of Public Finance and Accountancy. [www.tison-line.net]. Cook, P. (2005) *A Practical Guide for Local Authorities on Discretionary Income Generation* London: Chartered Institute of Public Finance and Accountancy. [www.cipfa.org.uk]

99 *Quality and Choice: A Decent Home for All – The Way Forward for Housing* 2000 London: Office of Deputy Prime Minister. [http://www.housing.odpm.gov.uk/information/index18.htm] *A Guide to Social Rent Reforms in the Local Authority Sector* 2003 London: Office of Deputy Prime Minister.

restricted to London and Durham, revenues being less than expected because more people than expected change transport mode or change time of travel (outside the charging period). Both authorities intend to increase their charging areas. A referendum in Edinburgh in early 2005 rejected congestion charges, perhaps reinforcing the reluctance of other city municipalities to actively pursue them. However, they may be more willing to introduce charges following the introduction of a nationwide scheme of road charging some time in the future. This scheme will be introduced subject to the outcome of trials in various local authority areas of alternative road pricing technologies, including satellite technology. It could monitor use of particular roads by individual vehicles and charge them accordingly and so allow a direct connection to be made between demand, charge, investment revenues and capital funding.

Variable charges for collection of household waste based on volume and/or weight could be used as part of a 'polluter pays' philosophy, the amount paid in charges being reduced if households participate in doorstep recycling schemes. A public education campaign reducing production of waste by increasing recycling will reduce the money raised from direct variable charges. Nonetheless, this is a desirable outcome, just as city road charges are successful if they lead to a reduction in traffic congestion and so raise less money than expected. Indeed, very substantial revenues raised from direct charges for collection of household waste would indicate failure to meet environmental, social and economic objectives and failure to change our waste-maker culture. In the meantime, new or higher charges could be levied for collection of bulk waste, removal of abandoned vehicles, etc.

Charges for use of sports and leisure facilities are already very well-developed but they could be increased to be more comparable with levels in the private sector and new charges could be developed, for example, for provision of personal training coaches. Culture and related services could charge for access to historical records and to special exhibitions at museums and galleries maintaining free admission to their main collections.

Fire and rescue services could increase their use of charges for non-fire fighting (special) services, especially for discretionary services provided to commercial organisations seeking to profit from them. These include charging insurance companies for the costs of dealing with non-fire related emergencies (e.g. road traffic accidents, releasing jammed lifts, lift rescues from silos and sewers), non-emergency calls (e.g. effecting entry to premises, pumping water out of flooded buildings, dealing with chemical spillages and other hazardous materials and for use of high-reach vehicles), fire safety training (provided to commercial companies, including North Sea oil companies), and humanitarian incidents (e.g. rescuing horses and cows from ditches, slurry pits and bogs, extraction from which requires use of heavy lifting equipment).

Police services could make more use of charges for crowd control at football matches, and festivals in public parks, or for late-night policing of 'alcohol disorder zones' in city centres with many pubs and clubs. Those organisations pay charges related to the number of officers required to provide the extra level of policing over the relevant time period. Charges could also be levied on companies receiving training in security and crime prevention and charges could achieve higher cost recovery ratios in providing improved services in respect of community safety, much like the fire service.

Non-core education user charges may increasingly be levied in the form of 'voluntary' contributions by parents to schools, for example, for special equipment. School meals services may have to raise meals charges (which cover little more than half of costs) if they are to meet the Department for Education and Skills 2005 guidelines in the *Healthy Eating Blueprint for England and Wales*.[100] Low-income parents whose children already receive free school meals would be

100 *Healthy Food in Schools – Transforming School Meals* 2005 London: Department for Education and Skills. [www.dfes.gov.uk/pns/Display PN.cgi?pn_id=2005_0044]

Police services could make more use of charges for crowd control at football matches and festivals in public parks or for late-night policing of 'alcohol disorder zones' in city centres with many pubs and clubs.

protected from higher charges. Charges could also be levied for non-statutory home-to-school transport.

Equity and charges

As already noted, the main argument against increased use of charges is that they increase inequality by excluding low-income groups too poor to pay them. This is only the case if charges are not means-tested. However, households whose incomes only just exceed the Income Support threshold will not be eligible for concessions based on receipt of that welfare payment. Moreover, administration of means-testing may be so expensive that charges cost more to introduce than the money they raise, plus means-testing is often so demeaning and intrusive of personal circumstances that it deters service take-up amongst the poor. In neither case do they create value for money.

These are serious objections to increased use of charges. However, they do not justify a blanket ban on consideration of further use of charges in respect of, say, discretionary services provided under the 2003 legislation (noted above) which are meant to increase availability of services and so facilitate choice. Moreover, these objections will generally not apply to charges paid by organisations rather than by individuals. Furthermore, equity is not a substantive issue in respect of, say, charges for optional bin cleaning services provided as part of the collection of household refuse or for non-statutory home-to-school transport.

Conclusions

The future of charges lies in the extent to which they are accepted by electorates in helping secure key social, environmental and economic objectives. Charging for services can encourage changes in behaviour in order to achieve those objectives. For example, charging motorists for use of roads can raise money for investments in public transport, so increasing the mobility of low-income groups which cannot afford cars. In encouraging a switch from car use to trains and buses, economic and environmental objectives are also achieved through the consequent reductions in congestion, pollution and accidents. Much the same can be said for charges for household waste collection in tandem with extensive doorstep recycling facilities.

There is a limit to the extent to which charges can be increased, not least because of equity issues. Nonetheless, service take-up is often proportionately greatest amongst affluent groups and constrained tax finances limit wider service availability. Moreover, it is unethical to adopt patterns of irresponsible behaviour leading to unwelcome environmental and social degradation and economic waste simply because services are free at the point of use. The generation of household waste simply because of failure to participate in recycling schemes and heavily congested roads due to unwillingness to use public transport are cases in point. There is evidence that charging for collection of household waste and for the use of roads makes people use these services more responsibly.

In the recast welfare state, charges are not simply a residual financial adjustment to local authority budgets. Instead, they have the potential to be a key instrument for delivering value for money and Best Value by distinguishing between the private and public good characteristics of services. They can also help deliver social justice by helping to target subsidy on those judged to be most in need of a service and yet least able to pay for it. They can also facilitate increasing choice within the public sector by helping make available the finance to provide discretionary services under the 2003 legislation.

To oppose all charges on equity grounds, or because they may raise little revenue, is simply not tenable and there is clearly considerable scope for charging strategies to be much more fully developed than is presently the case.

Three co-payment case studies

The following three case studies are designed to show different potential uses of co-payment. The first case study gives an example of how future technologies and health interventions could be made more affordable through co-payment. As new drugs and technologies become available, the public will expect to see them available on the NHS, but they may be precluded because of their lack of cost-effectiveness even though they may have some measure of clinical effectiveness. Co-payment could give patients more choice over treatments by letting them pay a proportion of the cost for these interventions while the rest could be funded by the taxpayer.

The second case study argues that access to a national school bus scheme is an essential part of fulfilling the goal of increased school choice and suggests that this can be achieved through co-payment. Parents who could afford it would be required to pay a proportion of the costs of the school bus, while poorer parents would be given a full subsidy to ensure equity of access. It is argued that this could also have the knock on benefits of reducing congestion caused by the school run and increasing safety. Once again, co-payment can have multiple consequences for the service in question.

The final study considers the introduction of a national road user charging scheme which the Government is currently considering. It suggests that co-payment could help to reduce demand for vehicle use at peak times and could increase revenue to pay for road improvements. Depending on the design of the charge, co-payment could also have environmental benefits. However, questions of equity remain important, as do notions of public acceptability, if the scheme is going to work in practice.

Case Study One: co-payment for a cervical cancer vaccine

101 Currie et al. Health Behaviour in School-aged Children (HBSC) study: 2001/2002 survey.

Sanofi Pasteur MSD is a supplier of vaccines in the UK and is currently in the final stages of developing a new vaccine against cervical cancer. Cervical cancer is caused by a virus called the Human Papillomavirus (HPV), which infects the majority of sexually active women at some point in their life. In some women the infection persists and leads to pre-cancerous changes and ultimately can progress to cancer.

HPV is highly infectious and starts to infect young people as soon as they become sexually active. Therefore, an effective vaccination programme must begin with universal vaccination of teenage girls before first sexual contact, probably at around 11 or 12 years old. Evidence shows that in England 40% of 15 year olds are already sexually active.[101]

Research has suggested that women in the UK are likely to show a high level of interest in the vaccine. Although the most effective time for intervention is pre-teens, there will inevitably be significant demand from older girls and women. Co-payment could provide a short term solution for a fixed period of time (until all women are vaccinated routinely) that would allow the widest access to the vaccine within a manageable budgetary framework.

Under this proposal there would be a free universal vaccination programme for all girls before they become sexually active, plus a catch-up period, as is the norm with vaccination programmes, for example offering the vaccine to girls up to the age of 16. A system of co-payment for the older age group would enable recipients to receive the benefits of the vaccine without the cost to the NHS becoming unreasonable. To ensure equity of access, women on lower incomes would receive the vaccine free of change.

There would be a number of benefits of introducing the vaccine in this way since it would allow government to balance public expectation and demand with the vaccine's individual and societal benefit. It would also prevent government having to choose between lowering costs by only allowing access to those for whom the vaccine would provide maximum benefit and allowing older women access to the vaccine but incurring large costs for the NHS. This would reduce pressure on GPs who would otherwise have responsibility for deciding on a woman's eligibility. Finally, it would ensure more equitable access for older girls and women.

Possible usage scenarios

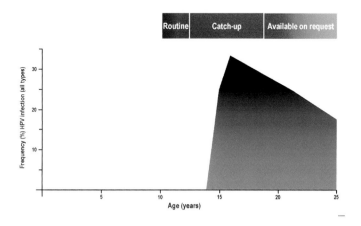

Hypothetical distribution of HPV prevalence in EU modelled on data available in the US and Canada [10]

This diagram shows how the frequency of HPV infection rises very sharply when girls become sexually active. The incidence peaks for girls at 16 before dipping quite dramatically. In this model routine universal vaccination would be introduced for girls between the age of 10 and 12. Those between 12 and 16 would be covered with a catch-up programme, and a system of co-payment would be introduced for those older than 16 who wanted the vaccine.

The use of co-payment in this circumstance could allow the government to manage a potentially difficult scenario – a sudden demand for a service. After a period of time, when all girls between the age of 10 and 12 are routinely vaccinated, the need for co-payment will disappear. Using co-payment in this way demonstrates that it need not be a blunt instrument, but can be used as a flexible solution to manage one-off peaks in demand for new technologies or services.

With thanks to Richard Stubbins, Managing Director, Sanofi Pasteur MSD

Case Study Two: co-payment for a national scheme of school buses

102 Sutton Trust, *Home to School Transport Survey*, February 2003.

103 SMF, *No More School Run*, June 2005

School transport in this country is patchy. Local authorities are obliged only to provide transport to children living either two miles (for primary pupils) or three miles (for older children) from a suitable school. Consequently, school bus services are generally only found in rural areas or serving faith schools.

Unsurprisingly, therefore, 20% of traffic in the morning rush hour is on the school run.[102] This has a negative impact on the environment, children's health and safety, and also wastes thousands of hours of parents' and other road-users' time. It also has a social cost: a lack of affordable transport means that children from poorer families are significantly less likely to travel to attend the best state schools.

In a joint Social Market Foundation/Policy Exchange publication, the Sutton Trust argued for the introduction of a national network of US-style yellow school buses, open to every pupil. These buses would help to improve safety and cut congestion, and, because they would serve a range of local schools, they would also give parents of all backgrounds increased choice over their children's education. Local pilots have already proved popular.

The cost of providing yellow-style school buses for all primary school journeys over one mile has been calculated at £184 million a year – compared to the calculated benefits of £458m.[103] If a proportion of current school transport subsidies (£60m) were applied, plus revenue raised under the current fare structure at 50p a journey (£41m), the cost would fall to £83m a year.

Co-payment in this case appears to provide a workable solution: every family would make a modest contribution to their child's school journey, except those children eligible for free school meals, who would travel for nothing. If this system were adopted at the same 50p a journey rate, the cost of primary school buses would fall another £44m to under £40m a year.

It is important to note that this is not a perfect solution: depending how the system would operate locally, there might be some families, particularly in rural areas or attending

104 *Putting the brakes on climate change: A policy report on road transport and climate change*, Julie Foley and Malcolm Fergusson, IPPR, October 2003

105 CBI quoted in House of Commons Transport Select Committee Seventh Report, March 2005

106 For a copy of his speech visit www.smf.co.uk

denominational schools, who would have to pay for a service they currently get for free. As with any system with a cut off point, there will also be some families just above the threshold for whom the sums involved will be difficult to manage.

But if free travel for all is not realistic, then co-payment is a good compromise, which is certainly fairer than current arrangements. If properly implemented, it would result in a better system which offers more choice to more people – either for free or at a modest cost – and could help to make a reality the economic, social and environmental benefits of yellow buses.

With thanks to James Turner, Research Officer, The Sutton Trust

Case Study Three: road user pricing

Since the mid 1980s, the average number of trips per person made by car has increased by 24% from 517 to 659 per year and distance travelled by car has increased by 61% from 388 to 624 billion passenger km per year.[104] The negative impacts of current levels of road use include economic, social and environmental damage. Approximately £20 billion pounds a year worth of time is lost through traffic jams and there is a reduction in quality of life for communities with heavily congested roads.[105] In addition, road vehicles currently account for 22% of all UK CO_2 emissions – the main gas responsible for the human contribution to climate change. Current trends suggest that its contribution will rise to 29% by 2010, damaging the prospects of the Government meeting its 2010 target to cut emissions by 20% compared to 1990 levels and eroding any carbon savings from increased energy efficiency. Recognising these problems, Transport Secretary Alastair Darling announced a debate in June 2005 on whether the Government should introduce a national scheme of road pricing.[106] One of the difficult issues if this goes ahead will be to balance the different objectives of a road user charge. It is right that the Government's primary objective for the charge is to reduce congestion on Britain's busiest roads, but it could also be used to make vehicle users responsible for an element of the environmental impact of their car use. The primary economic problem regarding road use is that the person making the journey does not face the total cost of each road journey. The cost of a journey is made up of private costs – time, fuel, and vehicle maintenance – and external costs – the infrastructure, the environment, accidents, and increased congestion. At the moment the road user only faces private costs. Calculating the external costs, however, will be quite difficult.

However, revenue neutrality would help the policy gain acceptability with motorists. Figures show that 47% of motorists would accept road charging if this leads to lower road tax.[107] But if motorists are really going to be convinced to change their behaviour in the interests of the environment, the total cost of car use has to be higher than at present. Moreover, there are good arguments for hypothecating revenues for better public transport. Furthermore, if fuel duty is cut, for example, to make the scheme revenue neutral, this would remove an incentive for fuel and engine efficiency. This would seem a backward move at a time when we need more measures to encourage greater fuel efficiency. From an economic perspective, therefore, charging for road use may be a more flexible way of pricing environmental externalities.

Ensuring that the scheme does not unduly impact on equity must also be considered. While those from poorer households tend to travel less by car and shorter distances, there will still be a significant minority for whom road user charging will present an additional burden and may impact on decisions about work or childcare. One answer to this is to hypothecate the charge, in the same way as is the case with the London congestion charge. The money could then be reinvested in public transport or in road maintenance, creating park-and-ride systems, or making road infrastructure expansion more environmentally friendly. This could have the added benefit of generating more public support for such a scheme because of the transparency between the charge and the use of the revenue.

The success of a national road user charge will depend on many factors, but introducing co-payment on a national scale

107
http://www.mori.com/polls/2005/detica2.shtml

could hold the key to reducing demand for travel at peak times, increasing revenue for road maintenance and new build, while also fulfilling a key environmental objective of decreasing harmful emissions.

SMF Publications

Reinventing Government Again
Liam Byrne and Philip Collins (eds.)
2004 marked ten years since the publication of Osborne and Gaebler's landmark book Reinventing Government. In Reinventing Government Again a number of authors assess the extent to which the ten principles for entrepreneurial government enunciated in the original are reflected in the UK today.

December 2004, £15.00

Too Much, Too Late: Life chances and spending on education and training
Vidhya Alakeson
This report argues that the link between educational attainment and family background will not be broken as long as the pattern of spending on education and training continues to offer a far greater public subsidy to tertiary rather than preschool education. The report proposes a reallocation of spending in the medium term in favour of children under five.

March 2005, £15.00

A Fairer Prescription for NHS Charges
Social Market Foundation Health Commission Report I
At present, even under a National Health Service (NHS) purportedly 'free at the point of use', many charges are levied. Many people have, for example, to pay for prescriptions, for dentistry, for eye testing and for spectacles. All these charges are subject to elaborate systems of exemptions and exclusions. Ministers maintain that the present level of charges is generally accepted and has stood the test of time. This report from the SMF's Health Commission leads to the opposite conclusion. They argue that the present system is a dog's dinner, lacking any basis in equity or logic and stuffed with anomalies and inconsistencies. The report recommends an overhaul of prescriptions to better reflect ability to pay and efficacy of the drugs prescribed.

June 2003, £15.00

No More School Run: Proposal for a national yellow bus scheme in the UK
The Sutton Trust
This report argues that a national system of school buses would have a number of benefits: lowering greenhouse gas emissions; improving safety for children; reducing truancy; and enabling the wider community to take advantage of a reliable source of transport. It also argues that if choice of school is to become a reality for everyone, an effective school transport system is required.

June 2005, £10.00

To the Point: A Blueprint for Good Targets
Report of the Social Market Foundation Commission on the use of targets
This report is a thorough examination of the Government's use of targets in four public services: education, health, housing and the criminal justice system. The report sets out the design flaws in the current targets regime but concludes that these flaws are the result of specific design problems. This report presents a range of practical proposals to improve the way in which targets are designed in the future. These are illustrated with a definition of a "good target", encapsulating the principles of how, and when, targets should be set.

September 2005, £15.00

Making Choice a Reality in Secondary Education
Claudia Wood
In this publication the Social Market Foundation argues that the Government's proposals on school choice need to be bold and integrated if they are to succeed – or else they risk making an already unfair education system even less equitable when it comes to underprivileged families. The report emphasises the extent to which the English school system has been blighted by inequity of access and outcome, and argues that extending choice to all parents could be the key to levelling this playing field.

October 2005, £10.00

User Charges for Healthcare
Social Market Foundation Health Commission Report 2D
This report considers the case for changing the current system of charging in the NHS in order to generate extra revenue. It concludes that charges should not be extended into most clinical and preventative services, but that there is no reason why in principle charges should not be extended to non-clinical services.

September 2004, £15.00